D1273184

NEW CHUM

JOHN MASEFIELD

NEW CHUM

New York
THE MACMILLAN COMPANY
1945

92
M396m

TO

MY WIFE

NEW CHUM

NEW CHUM

Welcome, stranger, to this place,
Where Joy doth sit on every bough.
WILLIAM BLAKE

I SET out to join H.M.S. *Conway* on a fine sunny morning a fortnight after the September term had begun. As I had been exposed to an infection of chicken-pox, the ship had refused to receive me sooner. The *Conway* autumn term always began very early, about the 9th; and in that lovely weather my extra fort-night of holiday had been welcome to me. Had I known what disadvantages it would bring me for the next two years, I should have changed my tune.

As I walked to the station, I thought with joy that that night I should be sleeping in a hammock over my own sea chest, which would contain not only the black-ing-brushes, with which I should be able to polish my own shoes, but my "knife, fork and spoon, with name engraved"; "a jack-knife with lanyard"; a pair of sea boots; Raper's Navigation and Tables, and many articles with strange names, a jumper, a pair of bluchers, white drill trousers, blue Crimea shirts, and one superfine uniform for Sunday. I have set down the things in the order in which they pleased my expectation; hammock and sea-chest certainly first, Sunday uniform last. I did not know what Raper's Tables might be. I think I expected some snug and neat kind of mess table, which folded up when the messmates had finished. I was thirteen years three months and three weeks old; expectation was lively in me; as someone says of Shakespeare, "he had the Phantsie very strong".

As I walked to the station on that very fine sunny September morning, an old man driving past me, half pulled-up, pointed with his whip to the northward and said: "There's a house on fire". Sure enough, a couple of miles away or a little less, a house seemed to be in a blaze. "That'll be about the Woncots," he added, driving on, with his eyes fixed upon it. I stared at the blaze for a minute, noticed that there was no smoke, and decided that it was only a window catching the morning sun. I have often seen it, since then, from the same point on a sunny morning. Yet there was a thrill in the thought that it might be a house on fire, and that at any minute, I might see a man gallop in with the news, and perhaps have the luck to see the engines go out, led by postillions, who could take any man's horses as they chose, as I had seen them doing, more than once.

Most of the railway journey, being new to me, was of

great interest; much of it led through beautiful country, with little rivers of delight. I was to see it often in days to come and to remember it well, for each station made a landmark. As I went, I kept thinking of my hammock and my sea-chest. Someone had told me that the ship's company might be rather rough and ready. Years before I had slightly known a boy who was now on board; he had answered my enquiries about her in a letter containing these words. "She is all right. On Saturdays we have no school, but scrub the decks, which is fine work. Mind you bring back plenty of tuck, as it comes in useful on board." I had brought plenty of tuck, and looked forward to no school and scrubbing the decks. If there were any roughness, it would certainly fall on a new boy, I thought. I should probably be made to sing or to dance naked or something of the kind; but even if I were, there would be a hammock, I should sleep in a hammock over my own sea chest, which would contain not only my blacking-brushes, with which I should polish my own shoes, but my "knife, fork and spoon with name engraved", my jack-knife with lanyard, a ditty-bag and housewife, a pair of sea boots and two pairs of sea boot hose. These matters, of which I knew not the reality, filled my mind with expectation. They were as the carrots with which the donkey is said to be lured forward; (he already having an inclination that way). If some who read, wonder that I ranked the jack-knife so low upon the scale, let them remember that most boys have had knives, and to themselves called them jack-knives, but that few have had a hammock of their own, marked with a special number, and still fewer a sea-chest, with a movable wooden till, and Raper's Tables, no doubt ready to unfold "for all the mess to dine".

I kept thinking of the ship's prospectus, and of an article about her in the *Boy's Own Paper* some years before. Thinking of what these things said, I knew that I was bound for a boy's paradise, where each little angel sat up aloft in white drill trousers, or, on Sundays, superfine uniform.

My knowledge of the sea and ships was elementary. In the last few weeks, I had learned starboard from port, and had taught myself, from some books for boys, how to tie a bowline knot and a bowline on a bight. I was rather vain of these knots, but was soon to learn, that sailors do not tie them in the ways displayed in the diagrams.

> "Alas, unconscious of their doom
> The little victims play."

For many years, I could repeat the names of the stations at which my train stopped, and describe with some fulness the scene from both sides of the railway. It was not a very long journey. In the early afternoon, the train drew out of a cutting to a level. There, to my right, for a moment, was an estuary, with mud-flats streaked with water, a city under smoke beyond, and in

4

the stream, in sunlight, headed to the first of the flood, were four black wooden ships of war, with white gun tiers and black ports, each fully-rigged, lying at moorings in line ahead. I knew that one of these was the *Conway,* I saw that one of them was a frigate; the three battleships seemed to me exactly alike. In a moment, the scene was hidden by the railway cutting. I had another glimpse of a muddy bay in the River, with a big steamer at a buoy; then the train entered the partial darkness of a covered way, with gleams of light and whitewash, and a strange noise, as of clanking milk-churns, a noise such as I had never before heard, which seemed to come from above and to be connected with the gleams of light. I was to hear this noise many times. It was the racket and clatter of Lairds' ship-building yards; men were riveting and hammering on a big ship's frame there.

A minute after this, the train drew up at the long platform of the terminus, and all set forward towards the sunlight of the exit.

As I came out of the station into the light, I saw in front of me, close to, beyond the wall of a warehouse, the masts of a splendid ship, known by me to be splendid, although I knew nothing of ships or splendour. They towered there, exquisite in line, noble in rake and in style, loftier than anything near-by, daunting, in their height, yet alluring; they were pinnacles which could be climbed. Ah, if I had known, surely I should have given the afternoon to a nearer knowledge of that

5

wonder. Seagulls were floating about, crying. She had a drooped house-flag at her truck.

I went down a sloping, covered pier to a landing stage, and thence to a ferry steamer, which almost instantly shoved off across the River. I looked for the first time at a busy seaport, and at that highway, then one of the most crowded in the world. There were docks full of masts all along the stream in front of me; there were docks and shipyards astern. Away up the River, in the dimness I could see the wooden men of war. The River there was at its brightest bustle with ferries and moving shipping, tenders going to liners, tugs, launches and dredgers, mud-flats, under big red sails, and water flashing in the sun. I remember quoting some childish tale to myself: "All too soon, the journey ceased" as we reached the Liverpool Landing Stage and disembarked.

There were then docks just behind the Landing Stage, the George's Dock and another. As we drove past these, I had a near view of the mizen mast of a ship, and noticed closely, what had long perplexed me, how the spanker gaff was supported at peak and throat. I know now that she was an old ship, for on her fore and main yard-arms she had iron fittings the use of which I could not guess. Very soon, I learned that these were studdingsail boom irons, no longer used, but not yet removed from some of the ships still plying. Soon, I was in Paradise Street (known in song), at the Sailor's Home, and going upstairs to the outfitting department, a big

6

place, where many seamen fitted themselves for the sea.

Along one side of the big well-lighted room was a show case containing gold chin stays and specimen cap badges, showing in the most beautiful colours the house-flags of all the ship owners of Liverpool. These miracles of art at once caught my eye. I suppose that there were a couple of hundred of them. In the next two years, I came to know many of these flags; for I never failed to re-visit that gay case when I was near that part of Liverpool.

In another minute, I saw my chest, with my name painted on it. I was bidden into a dressing-room, where my uniform suit was laid out ready for me to put on. I shed my own suit, and put on the uniform. I remember that the trouser buttons were arranged in a way unusual to me, but quite easy to master. The tunic or double-breasted, brass-buttoned, blue reefer coat was so beautiful, that its discomfort was not noticed. When in my uniform, I felt the pockets in coat and trousers; there was one, outer breast pocket in the tunic, none in the trousers; "only one pocket is allowed," I was told. Into this pocket, I put my regulation coloured handkerchief, my chest key, and the usual belongings of a boy; then I put on my cap, which also bore a shining badge, and with the instinct proper to all new chums, at all times, pressed it well down over my eyes. Having thus branded myself, and having been passed as dressed, the time had come to proceed to the ship and report myself as come aboard. Now was the woodcock near the gin.

As the *Firefly* took me to New Ferry, I saw the line of wooden men-of-war draw swiftly nearer. I thought that each ship had a number of boys aloft in the tops, and thought how lovely it would be, to stand on those airy platforms watching the shipping. What I saw were not boys, but the dead-eyes and laniards of topmast rigging. This I discovered for myself at once, for we passed close to the *Conway*, going under her stern, so that I could read her name. In a few minutes more the ferry was alongside her pier, and myself, my chest and tuck-box were bundled out. A cutter's crew (the port fore) were lying at the pier waiting for me. I was the unmistakable new chum whom they had been sent to collect, my tuck-box was probably tuck, about which they at once made up their minds; my belongings struck them as odd. However, they hove the things into the cutter, gave me a seat in the stern sheets, and seemed indifferent to me. As we shoved off, the starboard stroke oar politely asked me to move my foot along the stretcher, it being in the way of his own foot. I apologized for inconveniencing him, and moved my foot. I did not know at the time, that a foretopman's stroke oar is an important person, who does not usually speak to new chums.

I have no memory of that passage from the pier to the ship, except that as we came under the *Conway's* stern, to pull up to the starboard gangway, I saw her fore and main rigging manned, and the gangway filled with officers. In a minute, the oars were tossed, the boat fast, and myself received by the Captain, who said, that there was to be a boat race between the two maintop cutter's crews, one of whom had been waiting for the boat which brought me. In fact, even as he spoke, she was manned by her racing crew, and pushed off under tow with the steam launch for the starting-post. At this instant, the Captain perceived a first-class petty officer, known as Ambi, doing something hazardous on the top of the hammock netting. Even to me, it seemed that the boy was taking a chance. The Captain hailed him, saying: "None of that, now . . . Remember, the old sea proverb, 'One hand for the ship, but the other for yourself'. Hold on to something." Ambi did as he was bid, and almost at once the race began. It was the first boat race I had seen; it was a very close struggle, between two very fine crews; it was won by the starboard main by about a length. Later in the term, there being some doubt whether the boats were equally good, the same crews changed cutters and rowed the same course again, with the same result. I was much impressed by the frenzy of excitement in the ship's crew, and the desperate efforts of the rowers at the finish.

For about half an hour, I shared the courtesies accorded to those who bring new chums. I was shown the steward's pantry, all neat and shining, with the mess tins, butter, jam, and bread all ready for the morning's breakfast. The jam was offered me to taste; the Captain saying: "It's too sweet for me." I was taken aft upon the orlop deck, to the show hammocks, one of which was unslung and unlashed for me, so that I might see a mizen topman turn into it and make himself snug. I was shown my chest, tuck-box and tin-trunk all lying in midships near a grating. Then, the word was passed for the captain of the starboard focsle, who presently appeared to take charge of me. I was now a member of his focsle.

This captain was a big fellow, with a pale, smiling freckled face, and red hair; he was known on board as Red Swab. For some reason, never understood by me, he was not liked on board, but to myself, then and since, he has seemed a very good-natured, patient fellow, exceedingly well-chosen to take charge of a large batch of new chums. I liked him, and could not understand why seniors liked him less, or not at all. I think they were jealous of him.

Red Swab introduced me to the second captain of the focsle, who was known as Dick. He wore a thinner gold stripe upon his sleeve than Red Swab; he was a quieter and rather abler fellow, and like Red Swab, very well-chosen for his rate over the new chums.

Dick told me, that that part of the after orlop deck was the focsle's allotted home; that all their chests were there, and that at night their hammocks would be slung there. He told me that my number was 35, that I should find this number stencilled on my hammock down in the hold later on, and that I was to sling my hammock on a particular hook which he showed me. "You sling

the head of the hammock to the hook," he said, "and
for the foot, you will let down this iron crank from the
beams, and hitch the foot clue to it. Mind how you
unhook the crank, and be very sure that you hook it up
properly in the morning. You'll get some bangs on the
head from cranks before you've done."

In this, he told truth. I had some cruel bangs on the
head from cranks before I was much older; at the
moment, I was too full of joy (and of relief) to bother. I
had thought that the hammocks were slung from the
deck beams, some six feet six inches from the deck, and
had wondered how I was to reach up to sling the hammock and then to turn into it. Slung as they were, not
three feet from the deck, it would be easy to turn in, or
so I thought.

"Now, listen to this," Red Swab said. "The Fire
Alarm is 'the continued ringing of the ship's bell'.
When you hear the Fire Alarm at any time, day or
night, you will come at once here, fall in, and wait for
orders. Your job will be to bring up hammocks and
help to smother the fire, but, first, you will come here
and fall in. Remember that. If we are called to Anchor
Stations, supposing we are run into, or our moorings
bust, you will fall in here, likewise. Remember it." I
promised to remember, and have kept my promise.

I had been but a few minutes in this new world; I
had not seen much of the ship; I knew, however, that I
was on the orlop deck, and that this deck was usually
well below the water-line in an old man-of-war, and

seldom reached by the enemy's shot. It seemed a vast expanse; with a clear avenue of deck on both sides of the midship hatches, coamings, gratings and staunchions. Long rows of black sea-chests, with white, painted names, lay on both sides of the clear expanses; they were neatly aligned, "dressed-up to a deck-seam," as we called it.

My chest, being a late-comer, had been shoved into a sort of no man's land, amidships, just abaft the main hatch. Some P.O.'s and a lamb or two had their chests there. My nearest neighbour was a Quarter-Boy, with whom I very soon made acquaintance. He came down to his chest.

"Ah, chum," he said, "what's your name?" I told him.

"What's your Father?"

"I haven't got one."

"What's your Mother, then?"

"I haven't got one."

"Oh. You're a —— orphan, then; the same as me."

Someone from the port side, a tough party, asked what the chum had said.

"He says he's a —— orphan."

"Well, tell the —— orphan, he'll soon be sailor sick aboard this hooker."

One or two of them, attracted by the conversation, came down to look at the orphan. I had a chance to note my neighbour, and to see the state of his chest.

I learned later, that he was the dirtiest and most untidy member of the ship's company. I noticed at the time, that he had a look peculiar to old hands on board, of being up to every dodge, of having been battered by every possible tempest, and salted by every green sea. His uniform was as though he had been round the Horn in it. Unlike my other shipmates in that fine weather, he wore an old pair of sea boots. His chest was like a rag bag. His face was untidy, too. His mouth was out of shape, and one or two teeth were gone; he was ruddy and tanned and dirty; his hair came down under his cap. As he was chewing tobacco, he spat from time to time, with a sudden twitch of one side of his face. I had never before seen this done: it impressed me. As his chest was near mine, I saw him often during the first days, and came rather to like him, as a change. He had cleverness of a kind; it was directed to doing what he wished to do. He had a dislike of school work, and had with great skill contrived to dodge about half of all his possible lessons by going as launchee in the steam launch. Each one of us was supposed to have a week of being launchee; and those who liked the launchee life would sometimes buy the week of others, so as to avoid the lessons which the launch's trips caused her crew to lose. It was this continual service in the launch which made the man so dirty. Oil, coal dust, and the muck of the slip at low tide always marked a launchee's gear. This man looked like the tribal god of launchees.

He was low in all his classes, and, although old in the ship had never been promoted, and now never would be. He was a typical old hand, such as the ship produced, always in small numbers. Most of this, I learned later, of course; at the moment, he was startling, new, and very interesting; this was a shipmate.

(He sailed shortly after that coming Christmas, with some others of his term. His ship was lost with all hands somewhere at sea.)

The deck was pretty busy with men; it was a free evening and some were mooching or skylarking, some sitting in their chests, reading or sewing; some were netting hammocks, or watching those who were. Everybody who spoke seemed to shout, for the enclosed decks seemed to give resonance to all voices. I felt lost and out of it. What impressed me particularly was the bearing of so many of the men; they looked so old, so easy and so salt; they had such an air of the sea. Many of them looked as if they had been pirates all their lives.

I felt new and must have looked new. I *was* new.

I asked Dick, if he would like some cake. Dick said he would, so I opened my tuck-box and gave him some. Instantly, I found myself surrounded by a party of pirates, all total strangers to me, who laid claim on my bounty. "Say, chum, your spare cake," they said.

"Get out of it," Dick said. I rather liked being called chum by men so salt, though I was shocked by their asking; I thought that they might have waited for an invitation. However, I have always liked giving, so I gave. I found at once that this caused a run on the bank; instantly, I was beset. "Here, lock that box," Dick said, "you'll have nothing left for yourself in half a minute"; so I locked the box and the crowd dispersed. I had learned, in those few instants, that this was a community unlike any that I had known.

"Now," Dick said, "you had better take off that cap and those boots. You are a junior, that is, a first-year man, and can only wear that peaked cap when you go ashore. You will wear a working cap on board, and deck shoes. Let's have a look at your chest."

I opened my chest; Dick searched it with a practised hand; he produced a pair of black deck shoes, such as all wore on board, and then a working cap, with two black dangling ribbons and a little ball of wool on the top. I put on the shoes, then Dick said: "We wear caps all the time, except at prayers and school; you will wear your working cap until you're rated petty officer."

He left me at this point, and having looked a little at my chest, and discovered that *Raper's Tables* was the name of a book full of incomprehensible figures, I put on my working cap, ribbons, top knot and all, thinking that it gave me a really marine air, and set forth to explore the ship a little while it was still light.

"Hey, chum," a voice shouted, "where d'ye think you're going in that . . . rig? Come here." A couple of toughs had got hold of me in the starboard main, near the open space of the hold. One of them took my cap. "These things aren't allowed," he said. With a jerk, he tore off the ribbons, and pitched them into the hold; with another twitch he tore out the top knot, and flung

15

it at a passer-by. "There's your cap, chum," he said, "and another time you come into the main top just remember to ask leave."

The cap had now a central hole in it as big as a florin, where the knot had been. I noticed, then, that no working caps had ribbons or top knots, and that a good many had even bigger holes than mine. What was meant by coming into the main top and asking leave I did not know; I had heard or read, that the top was up aloft somewhere. I continued my journey forward towards a romantic looking curve in the bows. Two crossed ladders, leading upwards near this place tempted me to go up, to the next deck. I was in an extraordinary strange world, of interest and wonder; it was all noisy, exciting and incomprehensible. It had a strange smell, too, of fresh paint, tar, and bakery. Clean paint seemed everywhere.

The ladder had a rope handrail, finished with a handsome knot. As I came to the top of it, to the lower deck, I found myself abreast a big pump, unlike any that I had ever seen, being violently hove round by a party of foretopmen, whose coats lay piled on the coamings. One of these instantly hailed me. "Hey, chum," he cried, "you're the chum who gave us that run in the cutter just now. Come and give a poor foretopman a spell. Come on, now; off saddle and at it." I supposed that he had a right to order me. In any case, I wished to show a willing mind. I took off my tunic, and took his place on the brake (the port brake, facing aft). This was the first work I did on board. It was not very difficult in itself, but this was a very smart top, and all that they did they did with fire, and in pumping it is the pace that kills.

"—— it, this chum can pump," a man said. He was one of the second spell, waiting for his turn. "—— it, chum, you ought to take my place, after I helped to bring you aboard."

"That's right," another said, "give poor . . . a spell, after pretty nearly killing him in the cutter."

I was willing to oblige; and very sorry to think that I had nearly killed poor . . . by making him row me from New Ferry. I do not doubt that I should have pumped there until the tanks were full had not my old acquaintance, who had told me to bring back plenty of tuck, come by in search of me. "Come on, now," he said, "let this chum go. You've no right to work him like this before he's been an hour aboard."

"Get away with you," they answered, "the chum volunteered." However, I left the pump, and joined my acquaintance, who wore the broad gold stripe of a senior petty officer. He led me aft on the port side of the lower deck, where we continued to walk for a time, up and down, between the gun and the Second Officer's cabin. All was new and strange to me. The gun shone with gleaming metal of three different kinds. "It is a naval gun," my friend explained. "Some of the men here go into the Navy, and many go into the Naval Reserve, so they do a certain amount of gun drill."

17

In amidships on that deck near the main hatchway was a capstan, and on either side of it, still amidships, was a big old-fashioned ship's cannon. "Twenty-four-pounders," my friend explained. They were in the ship's main deck battery, when she was in commission.

I offered some of the tuck which he had advised me to bring; I never knew any *Conway* boy refuse tuck. He led me down to the orlop deck again, explaining the uses of things, and giving me advice. A maintopman, with a face like a big bath sponge, shouted out that my friend was forgetting all his old friends now that he had shipped his stripes. I could not see the point of the remark, because he was remembering me, whom he had known, slightly, long before. The opening of the tuck-box, as before, brought a horde of quite shameless beggars round me, all of them total strangers, all of them with strange cries of: "Your spare, chum," or "Give a poor maintopman something, who's been pumping his —— guts out." While we were busy thus, Dick and Red Swab caught me, saying that in a few minutes we should be hoisting the two cutters, and that there would be work for me to do. I could walk with my friend afterwards. Almost as they spoke, a shrill pipe blew on the deck above and somebody shouted something. "That is the pipe for it," Red Swab said, "Focslemen, reeve cutters' falls." I had not heard one word of the order, and knew nothing of what was meant, but Red Swab led me to the lower deck, well forward to a nook among the bitts. "This is a job you'll have to do every evening," he

said. "These are the leading blocks for the falls." He
showed me two great blocks, with pendants on them; a
port focsleman had already laid hold of one, I took the
other, and at Red Swab's bidding dragged it aft along
the deck, to a point near the quarter deck, where he
lashed it. He then showed me a rope, which he told me
was the cutter's fall; I had to poke the end through the
block and drag it forward as far as it would go. It was
beginning to be dim on board; the big battle lanterns
had been lit; and swinging copper lamps were being
placed on the other decks. A man with a pipe, standing
close to me, blew a blast and shouted something aloud.
"That is 'Hands, up cutter'," Red Swab said, as a rush
of men began. "You will clap on to the rope there, and
haul at the order." I caught hold of the rope, and envied
Red Swab his proud post at the big leading block; but I
felt that my own post was pretty fair, to be manning a
rope on an old man-of-war's deck. I was one of a ship's
company, about to haul a rope, to hoist a cutter. I
gripped the rope and clutched it to me, and instantly
felt a bang on my knuckles. "—— it, chum; buttons,"
someone said. "You're skinning my —— knuckles with
your buttons. Don't press against the rope like that."

I was abashed at the rebuke, but it had been deserved. My buttons were brass, of a bulgy make, with a
raised anchor on their surface. Often enough, similar
buttons were to scrape my own knuckles. I apologized
for my clumsiness, held my body away from the rope,
and stood there, in the dim line of the starboard watch

all gently heaving at the fall, waiting for the order. It came almost at once. 'Haul taut . . . Hoist away.' We bent our weights to the creaking fall and started to walk away with her. On the other side of the deck, the port watch walked with the after fall. No doubt, we could have run away with her, but that was not encouraged; we walked away with her, and those who reached the forward deck laid aft, tailed on again, and again set forward. I reached a point close to the capstan, when the order and pipe came: 'High enough.' At this, all the haulers ceased to haul; I stood with them, holding the rope. A man just forward of me on the rope, said, in a low voice in my ear: "When he says 'Light-to,' haul for all you're worth." I nodded, thinking that this was kind instruction. When 'Light-to' was called, I hauled for all I was worth.

Unfortunately, 'Light-to' means, fling the rope aft, so that those standing near the stoppers may have plenty of slack with which to belay the fall at the cleat. The starboard watch flung the fall aft, as always, with all the power of their bodies, and I, who was hauling hard against the strength of perhaps eighty men, went flying with it, violently banging into the double line of men, and receiving violent kicks and blows from those I hurt. I came down on to the deck with a bang, wondering what on earth had happened to me. I was more startled than hurt, and then, too, think: I had learned something. Somebody helped me up, and asked: "If the crutch of my trousers had given away." I was glad to be able to say "No". "Ah," he said, "my first night on board, I went spinning like that, and my trousers went in the crutch, where they generally do go, in a fall."

Dick and Red Swab now showed me how to unreeve the first cutter's fall and to reeve the second cutter's in its place. When this was done, we hoisted the second cutter. I had now learned, not to scrape men's knuckles with my buttons, and not to haul at light-to. The rather dim deck, the crowd, the strangeness, and to be hauling upon a rope in a ship, were all excitements which some men there meant to make more prosaic. We had lighted-to; someone had blown a peculiar blast which I knew later as a Pipe Down; the ship's company was dispersing. Suddenly somebody gave me a shove in the chest; I tottered back, and fell over a man behind me. I came heavily down upon the deck, and was kicked and punched by the man over whom I had fallen. I thought that I had knocked him down, and was about to explain, but he slipped away chuckling. He had crouched to upset me when his accomplice shoved. Dick caught me here. "Come along," he said, "you'll have to unreeve the fall and stow the lead block." One of my focsle to whom I had already taken a dislike, growled at me for not leaping to this work at Pipe Down, "leaving it all to him". However, as he had left it all to me, no great harm had been done. I dragged the heavy lead block to the nook in which it was stowed. Dick said, that this would be my task every evening, to drag out and stow the great block.

My friend presently came to find me and led me back to walk with him as before. New experiences were coming upon me every minute. I was not thinking of hammock, sea-chest, and the other wonders, now, but of being in a ship, close to hatchways, cables, ports, old cannon, and a brand new gun which fired a shell. In this ship, I was walking a deck in a space between real cabins. Suddenly a ship's bell, on the deck above me, made three bells.

"Three bells," my friend said, "half-past seven."

I wonder how many thousand times I have recalled those words at half-past seven in the evening, remembering how and where he spoke them, on the port side of the lower deck, abreast the main hatchway, as we walked aft towards the gun.

My friend was exceedingly kind and helpful. He told me much and gave me a lot of good advice. My acquaintance with him had been of the slightest and he was some years older than myself. He had been long on board and was eminent in the ship. He said that I "must expect to be put through it just at first, since they always roast new chums the first few days". I learned, too, that he was not in my watch, and that men in different watches (and of different terms and years) seldom met much. (I never walked with him again.)

I was then an eager swimmer, and longing to know what swimming I should have. "None from the ship," he said, "the tides are too strong, and the currents too dangerous. As a junior you'll get to the Liverpool Baths once a week, and as a senior, generally twice a week; and, of course, when we have a Liverpool Leave, that is, a whole holiday in Liverpool, we can have all day at the Baths."

"What are the Liverpool Baths like?" I asked.

"Well," he said, "you really would expect a place like Liverpool to have better baths. The George's Baths, where we go, are really very small. The Cornwallis Baths are better, but they aren't as big as you'd expect."

His words dashed some of my hopes, for I had been thinking that we should be swimming and diving daily from the ship. His judgments were over-harsh. I was soon to find, that the Baths of Liverpool, though not big, were beyond all my dreams of possible perfection: I have known none better anywhere.

I was so excited by the experience of being in a ship, that "being put through it" seemed a small price to pay. But what was this, about being roasted, the first few days? I had seen on the orlop deck the ship's furnace, now lighted to warm the sleeping deck; did he mean that I was to be roasted there? I had read how the wicked had roasted Tom Brown. My friend laughed, and said: "No, no; I mean they'll have you on toast, if they get the chance."

Honest mariner's fun, I hoped; all a jest; they would but poison in jest.

Suddenly, in the midst of our talk, eight bells were made above us; a long call of the pipe followed, with a shout of which I distinguished not one word. My friend said: "That is eight bells. Supper-time. I go to the petty officer's supper, in a special mess. I'll show you where you'll get supper, if you want any."

I could see, that the last pipe had caused a great commotion in the ship. Men were rushing about at speed, and already, on the deck on which we walked, men were producing rolls of fire hoses and trundling them along the deck. Other men were lifting down strong, square wooden bars from the beams, and fitting them to iron cranks; little squads of men with brooms were sweeping. My friend left me at a mess table set with hot broth and ship's biscuits, while he went off to more delightful fare. I did not want food on that day of excitement, but . . . this was ship's bread, the hard tack of romance; I had to taste hard tack. As I ate, bits of hard tack came at my head from various points, with well-practised aim.

An idle lounger sauntering by stopped as he passed me. He had a rather pleasant face and manner. "Ha, chum," he said, "I'm . . . of the port fore. I was in the cutter that brought you off this evening. Come on down and mooch a bit; we still have twenty minutes."

I was very glad of any friend; we went down together. He told me that the bars now fitted across parts of the lower deck were to support the maintopmen's hammocks. "Both the maintops sling on the lower deck," he said. "It's much the best place to sling; they're so near the lavatory basins in the morning. You'll find out all about that tomorrow."

When we reached the orlop deck, he linked his arm

into mine, in the manner of the twenty or thirty couples already slouching round the deck there. As we went slowly along, he said: "Top, please," at intervals, and told me to remember the places where these words had to be said. He said that while I was a new chum, and perhaps, too, while I was a junior, I had better use the full request: "May I come in the top, please?" and wait for an answer.

"It's all right with the mizen," he said, "but if you don't ask leave, the main may go for you with sea boots, and the fore will go for you with brooms."

"Oh . . . and another thing," he added. "Never get into one of these orlop deck ports or sit anywhere on this paint-work. This is the foretop deck, and the foretop don't allow it. If they catch you, they'll come down on you with brooms and you may get knocked about."

My heart warmed to this friendly guide. He had been one of the crew which had brought me off, yet he had put in no plea for tuck, on the ground that he had pretty nearly wrenched his guts out, shipping my —— dunnage for me. I wanted to give him some tuck; so, watching for a smooth, when there seemed to be few pirates cruising, I brought him some from my box, and we mooched on.

Suddenly, I heard voices shouting my name. "That is a call for you," my guide said. "You must shout: 'Where away?' " I did.

The voices answered: "Lower deck. Main hatch."

My friend said: "You must answer, 'Orlop deck. Port main'." Again I obeyed.

Two young men came hurriedly down the ladder to us. "We've been yelling for you this last ten minutes," they said. "Why the hell can't you answer. The Nurse wants you in the sick bay. You've not been measured for bathing drawers."

Green as I was, I had been warned against this, and my friend gave me a pinch on the arm. "Buck up, now," the young men said. "Nurse is waiting. Off with you." I said, that I should not go. "All right, my joker," they said, "Nurse will report you at Rounds. Don't try to sneak out of it by saying that you haven't been told; you have. You'll look —— odd at the bathing-drawer parade on Sunday, if you haven't got your pair."

When they had gone, my new friend told me, that of course it was a try-on, that new chums were often fooled in that way, and did go to the Nurse. "They'll very likely try to send you later on, to the Master-at-Arms, to be measured for your cutlass. Don't go to do anything, or get anything, unless your P.O.'s order you; then you will know it's all right."

A few minutes brought half-past eight, and the loud (but to me incomprehensible) call of hands to Divisions. "Now we shall have to fall in, to get our hammocks," my friend said, "you will fall in over there. Good night and remember, that if you are in trouble or want anything, you just come to me. I'm . . . of the port fore. You'll easily find me in the port fore."

I was touched and charmed by his kindness; there were always many friendly men like this on board, who remembered their own first joinings. I saw him several times during that term, but we were in different watches, and that was usually a bar to friendship. Years later, when I was rowing on the Hudson, near the Palisades, he suddenly hailed me from the shore, at a time when neither of us could stay long to talk. His ship was lost with all hands soon afterwards.

As he left me to go to his Division, I was caught in a rush of men coming down the main hatch. All hands seemed to be at skating speed, going at a rush, with calls, cries and snatches of song, about a hundred and eighty of them, now darting out and across to shake a friend's hand and say "Good night", now catching a chance to shove somebody into somebody else. In the friendliness of the instant, one or two total strangers shook my hand and wished me "Good night", which I thought extremely nice of them. My head was in a whirl at the newness of everything, but I had begun to understand, that this was one of the things which had to be done quickly. My new guide and Red Swab had both told me where I should have to fall in; indeed, both Dick and Red Swab were looking out for me. Red Swab shoved me into my place between 33 and 37 and asked: "Do you know your left hand?"

"Yes. This."

"You're sure of it?"

"Yes."

"Then you do know *something*. Well, when I give the order, 'left turn; right-about-wheel; quick march', mind you turn to the left, and follow your leaders down that open hatchway there into the hold, to get your hammock. Do you know what dressing-up means?"

"Yes. Getting into even line."

"Right. When the order comes, to dress-up to a deck seam, see you do it."

Dick came up to us. "Do you know your left hand from your right?" he asked.

"Yes; he knows his left hand," Red Swab said. "The first chum this term who does. I suppose, like the rest, he'll forget it when the time comes."

"Now look," Dick said. "When the Officers begin to come round with the lantern, you must hold out both your hands like this, palm downwards, till they have passed you. As they come abreast of you, you must call your number aloud. You know your number?"

"Yes. Thirty-five."

"Do it again with your hands out."

"Thirty-five."

"Don't forget, or lose your head, or do anything silly now. They won't bite."

I promised to try.

Dick, like all the other petty officers, fell back into line amidships, facing us. The ship's company, focsle-men and topmen, stood well back towards the ship's side. The chatter and babble died away. The Chief Petty Officer came aft, calling for a Still. The Captain of the Hold joined him, holding a lantern. The Officer came down the after-hatch to them, called us to attention, bade us dress to a deck seam; our line shuffled up, stiffened, held out its hands, palm downwards, and was silent. The Officer made some jovial remark to the lantern bearer, and at once began to move forward along the line of the starboard watch. The Captain of the Hold preceded him, a seam or two nearer to us, holding his lantern so that the light fell upon each boy's face in turn.

It was intensely interesting to me, who saw all this for the first time. I had asked my neighbours why we held out our hands; one of them said, "to show whether they are clean"; the other said, "for the Officer to shake when you say good night". I noticed with all my attention, and a well-dissembled squint, that the Officer did not shake any pair of hands, nor wish anybody good night, nor, as far as I could make out, did he look at the hands. He eyed the faces keenly, and asked after every missing number. The holding out of the hands was an old naval custom, devised, perhaps to stop any holding of weapons as an Officer passed; perhaps, as a rough test of sobriety.

I called my number without mishap or comment. As the Officer passed on to the foretopmen beside us, Red Swab turned us, and bade us quick march into the hold. Our leading numbers moved off at a very quick march; I saw them fling themselves down the ladder with a rush. "Buck your stumps," Red Swab called. My neighbour said: "Run, when you get down, or the foretop will run over you." With this threat in my ear, I rushed down the ladder into a narrow, ill-lit wooden passage which sloped towards a better-lit more open space. I was now beneath the water-line, in a strong medley of smells, such as must, damp, dry rot, tar, want of ventilation, cellar, sour canvas, all over-topped by what I soon came to know was bilge water.

Though my fellow focslemen were rushing from me, and I myself, the last of their party, was rushing after them, I did not rush fast enough, for at my heels came the foretop charging, with the war-cry "gangway for a smoker", and knocked me flying to one side. I picked myself up, and reached the main open space of the hold, where I could see great water tanks in the bordering dimness, and in the midst a confusion, of officers of the hold with lanterns, and hordes of rushing boys seeking and snatching hammocks from the racks in which they had been stowed. I had sometimes seen a disturbed ant nest, with many ants in excitement rushing to carry away cocoons. This scene was like that. Men were seizing the hammocks, heaving them on to their shoulders and hurrying off with them; men still charging down from the deck above were rushing into the stream of those going and obstructing their path. Men at the racks were calling: "Anybody seen 57?" or some other number. Men were swearing at being collided with, at not finding their hammocks, at the want of light, and at the new chums who always got in peoples' way. At every minute more men came rushing; the swearing and shoving grew. I had never looked for a hammock thus. I knew my hammock's number, but not where it would be, and with everybody in a hurry I knew not whom to ask. The light was poor. The numbers on the hammocks were not always very plain; as the painted oval number patch was sometimes worn or smudged, or perhaps half-covered by a turn of the lashing. I asked a man where I should be likely to find 35, he said, the Nurse had taken 35 for a small-pox case; I had better run and ask her if it had been fumigated. Somebody who had heard this answer, asked me where I had put it that morning. I said, I had not yet had it. "I don't suppose it's been issued yet, then," the man said. "You'll have to run up to the galley and ask the hammock steward."

I did not know where the galley was, but no doubt I should have gone, had not Dick appeared, like a good angel, to say: "I expect your hammock will be up against the end of the rack there, as it hasn't been used yet this term."

It was at the end of the rack, but I could never have hove it out by myself, and when I had it, a tight, hard roll, wrapped with lashing, and much longer than myself, I could hardly carry it. With Dick's help, I got it on to my shoulder and went tottering with it to the main hatchway, up which all the men were hurrying with their loads. The hammock had a dreadful tendency to fall off my shoulder, and everybody, it seemed,

had a dreadful tendency to bang into me, and then to
—— my new chum's eyes for being so —— clumsy. Still,
they were bent on reaching the deck above, and what
with oaths and shoves, and promises that they would
make Red Swab make his —— focslemen buck their
stumps in future, they sent me staggering up past the
iron gratings on to the orlop deck. This deck, when I
reached it was completely changed from what it had
been a few minutes before. Now, it was a long array of
swinging hammocks, spread with bedding and busy
with men rapidly slinging, unlashing, or making their
hammocks. There was a babble of chatter, a great hurry
everywhere, and the harsh noise of the lashers being
rapidly scraped upon the canvas; all the time, too, men
were trotting past with more hammocks, just as though
a hammock were an air balloon. I was still tottering
with mine, and those who saw me totter did their best
with a shove or two to make me totter better. Still, I
reached my crank; there was my hook on the stringer
near the port, and there was my crank, which I unhooked little as I was, without bringing it down on my
head. Now, to my joy, Red Swab told my next door
neighbour, 33, to see that my hammock was slung and
unlashed. I was able to do the unlashing myself; there,
within, were blankets, counterpane, mattress and
pillow, all so neat. Red Swab again came round. "Are
your sheets in your chest?" he asked. "Where are your
sheets?"

Alas, I had not the regulation sheets, but had

brought some sheets with me. "In my box," I said. "My sheets are in my box."

"Get them out; quick, then," Red Swab said. I did get them out, from that stowage place behind chests where my tin trunk had been hidden. Alas, the sheets were four together, in one big bundle. I brought out the bundle, which Red Swab shook adrift.

"What in the wide earth have you got here?" he asked.

"Sheets."

"Battleship's mainsails, more like. Look at them."

He shook the bundle again, and loosened it up. The sheets grew bigger at each touch; he shook one reasonably clear; it was new, coarse, and intractable; and now that the hammocks were slung, there was little room.

"Did you ever see such sheets?" Red Swab asked. "You can't use these in a hammock; each one of them's about four times too big."

By this time, most men had slung and prepared their hammocks; the bulk of the starboard watch was passing aft to the hatchway, expecting the pipe to Prayers. In a ship, where all is formal, neat, and ordered, anything untidy or unusual catches the eye at once. Men could not help noticing the spread of linen; they paused to watch, and of course remained to mock.

"Go it, Red Swab. Your spare maternity hospital."

"Focslemen, make all plain sail."

"Look at these sheets the chum's brought. Golly, chum, do you sleep five in a bed at home?"

33

"What on earth possessed you to bring these, chum?"

"Did the little sailor boy expect his nice double bed, then?"

By this time, the coarse shaken out linen was in a kind of pyramid. A pipe blew, and somebody shouted yap.

"We must leave it for now," Red Swab said: "there's Prayers."

He told me to cut along, up to Prayers, saying, that he would try to fix me later. I left my hammock slung at its crank and the pile of linen partly in the hammock, and the rest on deck.

I was very unhappy at the jokes about the sheets. I had looked forward to having a hammock all my own; alas, it seemed no great catch. These sheets might be remembered against me for the next two years; they might bring some loathsome nickname upon me, and blast all my prospects in the bud. However, here we were at Prayers, sitting on a row of forms, myself in the front row; the Officers and Masters aft; the Chaplain in a chair, and a petty officer reading a lesson. When the lesson was read, we knelt on the deck while the Chaplain read a prayer for us, and others, less godly, pricked the new chums with pins.

After Prayers, when we all stood in ranks, some Officers made brief reports to the Captain; we were then dismissed by tops. Half the men, as they moved swiftly off the deck were already undressing, undoing buttons, untying ties. Red Swab made me rush along the lower deck and down to my hammock. "Get undressed," he said, "Dick and I will try to get your sheets straight."

When I reached my hammock, it was, of course, flat on the deck, but Red Swab reslung it for me. I marvelled at the way in which men were skinning themselves of their clothes. Why did they hurry so, I wondered. But as Red Swab seemed to want such speed from me, I tried to be quick, with the unaccustomed clothes. My captains had decided, that perhaps one of my sheets, folded roughly into four might conceivably serve for one night; the other wilderness of linen would have to be shoved out of sight somewhere.

It seemed, that we had only been on the orlop deck a minute, when a man blew a pipe and shouted yap again.

"That's Prayers," Red Swab said, "kneel down and say your prayers."

I did as bidden; everybody knelt; I was not in any mood for prayer, nor was any such mood on the deck; everywhere, there was a rustle and a stealth of men swiftly undressing and getting into pyjamas. In about twenty seconds, another pipe and yap ended Prayers and the rush of undressing redoubled. Some men were in their hammocks within twenty seconds of the pipe. I soon learned, that it was a nightly contest, man against man, top against top, to see who could turn in quickest. I was not turned in, nor was my hammock fixed so that I could turn in. "It's no good," Red Swab said. "You must turn in as it is. I've got to report you turned in. We'll try to get you fixed after Rounds."

I turned into my over-beddinged hammock, which out-bulged at every move I made. I was most uneasy. These sheets had upset everything; I wondered if I should ever hear the last of them. Qualms beset me, whether I should not presently be roasted at the furnace a few yards from me, in midships. Night would be the time for roasting, I judged; night, when the officers were turned in, and the new chum had scant protective clothing. Other qualms came: In this queer world, might it not be that there would be a bathing-drawer parade on Sunday? Had I defied authority in refusing to be measured? What if there were such a parade, and I appeared the one shameless among the many modest? I should look worse than Adam and Eve and for a worse reason. I had real qualms.

All the same, the scene was new, wonderful and thrilling to me. I was in a ship on a deck in a hammock. I was one of a crew, one of a watch; that was a hatchway, those were chain cables. The deck was lighted by oil lamps. I could look fore and aft across long lines of hammocks with men in them. On the port side were similar lines; everybody seemed talking.

Now, on the port side, I saw Red Swab and others moving aft. An Officer was there; the talking suddenly stopped. I saw Red Swab and the petty officers with him moving aft, bareheaded, towards the Officer; they were making special reports, to assure him that the ship was ready for any emergency the night might bring. In a minute, they were moving back to their Divisions, where they stood to attention, bareheaded.

The man in the hammock forward from me had been mocking my sheets at intervals; he now told me that I should catch it, when the Officer spotted them at Rounds. I asked what I should catch. He said: "You'll go on the report at least."

My heart sank at this.

The hammock slung abaft mine had been slung and made before I had brought mine from the hold. It was not yet occupied. I asked my neighbour whose hammock it was. He said: "H.B.'s!"

At this there came a pipe and yap, followed by absolute silence for Rounds. The Officer, with a lantern-bearer and others, moved swiftly round the deck. In a minute, he had passed along the port side, and was coming aft towards me. I thought: "Now I shall catch it, and go on the report at least, whatever that means." I heard him say "Good night" to some men, and question one or two others. Nearer and nearer he came; then he was there. He eyed my unhappy sheets with some surprise (or my sad mind made me think he did). "That boy's furl seems to be all bunt," he said; the lantern-bearer laughed; then they passed on and away.

Red Swab and Dick came over to me, when the party had left the deck. "You must stay as you are for to-night," they said. "We can't do anything more with these sheets. We'll dump the rest of them behind chests until tomorrow."

I asked if I could get up before the regulation time, of six-thirty?

Red Swab said: "No. It's strictly forbidden. And you mustn't even turn out, now or at any time, without asking my leave. Even if I'm asleep you must ask my leave and heaven help you if you wake me. In the morning, you'll stay turned in till the pipe goes. You'll not want to turn out earlier, when you've been a month aboard. Now, good night to you."

The two went aft to their own hammocks, where they slowly undressed, bandying chaff with some neighbouring P.O.'s, their cronies.

I was sitting up uneasily in my hammock, wondering how I was to tuck my bedding round my legs in the easy manner of my shipmates, and too much interested in the strange scene to be thinking of sleep. My neighbour, after some remarks which he may have judged to be witty, about my sheets, was talking to the man slinging on the other side of him, when a man came down the ladder opposite, said "Good night" to a man slinging in midships, and came straight to the waiting hammock beside mine.

"So this is H.B.," I thought.

He wore the broad gold stripes of a first-class P.O. and I had already learned that such men were of extraordinary importance in the ship, and that new chums like myself were just things for foretopmen to knock about with brooms. He had a somewhat pale, merry and thoughtful face; straight, black hair and much decision in his movement. I liked his looks, and took to him. To my astonishment, he was exceedingly friendly. "Hullo, chum," he said, "I was beginning to wonder if you were ever going to join. But what's the matter? You seem to be all fine linen, more pride than profit."

"I'm afraid I've brought the wrong sheets."

"That'll be uncomfortable for tonight. But I'll tell you what to do. Go tomorrow to the Gunner, in the Gunner's office, and say you've brought the wrong sheets. He'll send to the Sailors' Home for hammock sheets for you. You'll have them on Monday morning."

I had not much pocket money, and said, that I couldn't pay for them.

"You won't have to. They are paid for. They are part of your kit on joining, like your chest and uniform. You can take these big sheets home, when we break up."

"Do you really think I could get the proper sheets?"

"Of course you can. If not by Monday's post, they will bring them on board when they come on Tuesday."

From the very first instant, this fine fellow brought cheer to me. My heart rose. I forgot my troubles, and began to watch the strange scene about me.

Now that Rounds were over, there was a certain movement about the deck. Red Swab had said that the rule was to turn in and stay turned in, and not to turn out without leave; that rule held good for new chums, and partly good for juniors; seniors and P.O.'s lived by

laws of their own. A few seniors in pyjamas came sauntering by, on one pretext or another, to chaff, to say
good night to some friend, or perhaps to make some
arrangement about the next day's work. Some of these
eminent men paused to say good night to H.B., who
seemed to me to be exceedingly popular and subject to
no law whatever. He undressed leisurely, and sometimes stood at the foot of his hammock making signals
with his arms to unseen friends across the deck, in the
port watch.

When he was dressed in his pyjamas, he laid himself
in his hammock, on the top of his bedding, and began
some odd acrobatics with his legs. He waggled them
this way and that, now singly, now both together, with
the most fascinating skill. I wondered what the devil
he was up to.

After a while, he sat upright, and peered across to
port. "I'm doing semaphore," he explained, "semaphore with old P. . . ., across in the port mizen, there.
Watch him answer, now."

I watched, with interest. Across the deck, to port,
two pyjamaed legs rose above a hammock and jerked
out a message. "That is 'Jam. More jam'," H. B. told
me. "Now I must acknowledge and pipe down."

He waggled a brief message, then straightened his
bedding, and turned in. "Now, then chum," he said,
"do you know any ghost yarns?"

As it happened, I knew a good many of different
kinds, possibly some hundreds, with which I had scared

my childhood whenever I had had the chance. I said that I knew some. "Right, then," he said. "Heave round and tell me some." He settled his pillow on the edge of his hammock, and turned towards me. With some care, lest I should fall out on deck, I turned towards him and began my ghost yarn. The ship's rule was not against talking, but against making a noise. As we were only a yard apart there was no need to speak loud. Our neighbours right and left settled to sleep. H.B. was a good listener; he loved ghost stories, and had a pretty taste that way. I have often thought of him since then, of his clever merry face, poised on the hammock edge, making me spout tale after tale.

Though I was much too excited to wish to sleep, I wondered when the lamps would be put out. I asked H.B. about it: "When will it be 'Lights out'?" He said: "We never have these lights out. We're in a fairway; we may be run into any night, or the ship may take fire, or the moorings part. We should be in a mess, if we had to turn out in the dark, to go to Stations. These lamps will burn all night. It keeps people awake at first, but you'll soon get used to sleeping in the light. I suppose, we'd better be thinking of sleep ourselves. Thanks for the yarns. You must spin me some more tomorrow night. Good night, chum."

He held out a hand for the usual ship's handshake, and rolled himself up for the night, in a way not possible for me in my wilderness of sheet. I did my best to roll up, but a very little rolling almost brought me to rolling out. The ship's company was mostly asleep by this time, but there were little scufflings here and there, and also sharp authority: "Who's that there, playing the fool? Stand up there, Pipsqueak. Take my hammock for a week." Once, as I remember, there came protest from Pipsqueak, with the result that he got the hammock for a fortnight. I was too new, then, to know what these punishments meant. I was much puzzled, excited and confused. It was thrilling to be in a ship, in a hammock, one of a crew, in a ship which might be burned down or run into, from which we might have to take to the boats, a ship in which a watch was now set, lest one of these things might happen. But, even so, I was acutely uncomfortable; my bed wobbled if I wobbled. The deck was lighted, and I was unused to sleeping in the light. Then, as the noise of the ship almost ceased, I became conscious of a plaintive strange whimpering noise, as of someone sobbing with maudlin tears within six feet of me. This was the tide going past the gangway on the other side of the plank; in fact, I was not certain, that it was not the tide coming in, as a leak; for I had read of such things, and of sailors suddenly finding six feet of water in the hold. Gradually, my fears dwindled, my dislike of the lamplight ceased to trouble me; I fell asleep; I imagine, not for very long. I was aware of something shaking, something jarring, then something rapidly falling; and as I woke I found that it was I who fell; my hammock and I came bang upon the deck. I had been "let down". It was only possible to let

down from the foot, and apart from the sudden shock
no harm was done. Unfortunately, I did not then know
how to sling a hammock so that it could not be let down.
I reslung my hammock as well as I could. I saw no trace
whatever of the man who had let me down. I turned in
again, and tried to sleep. It was a most uncomfortable
night. The watchman came round once or twice, to
have a look at the furnace, and to refuel it. To this day
the screech of a shovel entering coke reminds me of my
first night on board. I saw the watchman from time to
time; he was an old sailor, who looked about him along
the deck at each visit, for anything that might be amiss.
After his visit, I would try to sleep, but my hammock
was not a place for rest. I was near the starboard com-
pressor, and from time to time one or other cable
clanged its swivel with a noise like the trump of doom.
I did not know what it was, but it made me leap whenever it happened. I thought it was the cable breaking,
and that I ought to go to Anchor Stations. Everything
in my day had been unaccustomed, exciting and amaz-
ing. Surely, these sailors were the salt of the earth. In
my few hours aboard, I had learned, that first-class petty
officers were almost people from a better planet, yet
here was this H.B., plainly a superior first-class petty
officer, treating me like an equal, and taking all the
points of my ghost stories just as my best friend would
take them. Then that man . . . , of the port fore, who
had taken such trouble with me just before Divisions
. . . where should I find his like? True, I had been a

little shoved around, or so; I had expected as much, and a lot more. What was that, when compared with my luck in finding two such friends in my first four hours on board? Then, to crown all, I might have proper sheets by Monday's post, or certainly by hand on Tuesday. On the whole, though I was out of my depth, I was hopeful of finding footing.

Though the ship settled somewhat gradually to sleep, it woke with a jump at half-past six, when an Instructor came down a hatchway blowing the long triple wailing pipe, and following it up with the cry of "All Hands", and various odds and ends of "Out you comes", and "Heave out, there; out you sleepers, hey", as he went along the deck. On the deck above, someone urged up the maintopmen. The ship hove out of hammock almost as one man, with a great clank of cranks. Dick was there to see me up, almost before the pipe had ceased. "Get your shirt and trousers on," he said. "Be quick. And get your sponge-bag and towel ready. Quick, now. You'll have to rush to the lavatory, the instant Prayers are piped down." He himself was moving swiftly; everybody was moving swiftly except H.B., who was one of the gods of that little world, and could take his time. I put on trousers, shirt, socks and shoes faster than ever in my life. My washing things were ready at my side, when the sharp pipe and bark for Prayers went. The ship fell pretty still, but not many prayed. All of my watch who could do so unobserved were creeping on hands and knees under hammocks towards the hatchways for a desperate rush to the lavatories, to bag a basin, or two, or three the very instant 'prayers' ended. There were only seventy-two basins altogether and about eighty or ninety boys were dismissed to them at a time. There were in fact "more days than sausages": a basin was a prize. Now the lavatories were forward on the lower deck. Sleeping where we did, we new chums were certain to reach the lavatories last and a basin, to us, was the greatest possible prize. In an instant, the pipe stopped the private praying; there was a shout (quite unintelligible to me at that time) "Starboard watch to the lavatory. Port watch, lash up and stow." Long before the words were uttered, the starboard watch was dashing away in its race. I was near the main hatch, and did not do so badly, but as the maintop was already on the lavatory deck, and the foretop had a start of fifty yards, and the mizen and many supernumeraries were better placed than I, every basin was full long before any of the focsle got there. It was a pleasant scene of stripping and splashing, but not a place of welcome to a new chum. "Please, may I use this basin?" I asked. "Use this basin?" was the answer, "—— it, you don't seem to want much. Get to hell out of it."

Several basins seemed disengaged. I asked for others. I found that the really smart hand liked to seize three basins; one to soap in, one to rinse in, and one for a general wallow, or to give to a friend. In nearly every case, he had a friend depending on him, and the basins, when used were usually kept for the friend. I went up and down, hoping to find a place; sometimes asking, if I might have a basin when a man had quite done with it. Some men scooped water in my face, some flung wet sponges at me; and remarks passed, "The —— new chum wants a basin."

I dare say, that in my ignorance I asked eminent men, senior P.O.'s and so forth. As they were all in shirt-sleeves or stripped to the waists showing no gold lace stripes I could not tell how eminent they were. One man said: "There are lots of basins over to port," so I went to the port side, where by this time the congestion was made greater by the smarter hands of the port watch, who had stowed their hammocks. Here, I soon found my error. I happened upon members of the port watch, who very soon enlightened me. "What are you doing over to port? Keep to your own filthy side. —— it, these new chums seem to think they own the ship."

I went back to starboard, and oh, how I envied the big men, the seniors, the P.O.'s and old salt toughs, who laughed, chaffed and wallowed in the smart basins up by the manger. There was a big maintopman, one of the morning cutter, naked, wallowing, and singing a song, which I remember to this day. It was not much as poetry, still less as criticism of life, but, oh, how it showed an ease of spirit which I longed to have, and hadn't. A pipe blew, and a shout followed. I did not know what it meant, till someone said: "—— it, chum, you'd better buck your stumps and get washed. That's the pipe for you to lash and stow. Why the hell haven't you washed yet?"

There was Dick, asking the same question kindly. "It's too bad," Dick said. "Let him have a basin, Frog's-Guts; the kid only came aboard last night." Frog's-Guts was a big fellow, marked with small-pox. He had been born in the East somewhere, so it was said, and there had small-pox as a child. The markings on his face perhaps suggested frog-spawn to a lively fancy and perhaps frog-spawn was supposed by the ignorant to be guts. Dick had been in the maintop with him, and of course could call him Frog's-Guts, which would have been suicide for me. He was a very clever and a very decent fellow; he gave a pitying smile and allowed me to use a basin, while Dick stood over me and told me to hurry. "Buck up, now. You've got your hammock to lash. Never mind the suburbs; just wash the central square."

I neglected what suburbs I safely could; and then Dick hurried me down.

When I reached my hammock, nearly all the hammocks to port had been cleared and stowed. All along my side of the deck, men were working with what seemed deliberate ease, and was really masterly smartness. They were at various processes; making their beds, rolling their bedding, setting it, rolled, lengthwise in their hammocks, clearing the lashings, or passing the seven turns; or dropping the lashed hammock to the deck, twisting in the clues, shouldering the neat bundle and running off to stow it in the hold. All about me was

47

the rattle of lasher-ends hitting the deck, the grunt of cranks being hooked up, and the harsh scrape of lashers against canvas.

I had seen the thing done, the evening before; it had seemed easy. The men near me seemed to find it easy, bedding and lashings seemed to answer to a touch. H.B.'s hammock was gone. My other neighbour told me to "make" my hammock, and then roll the bedding tight. Now the real horror of my sheets began to dawn upon me.

I had slept in only one of these misshapen things. Dick and Red Swab had somehow doubled it for me, but for little me to double it for myself, to smooth it out, and make it lie nicely over my hammock was beyond my skill. My sheets had been noticed, the night before, now, they became a sort of public circus. Not even the oldest seaman there had seen such sheets. Men gathered at my crank to watch me. "Do note the sheets this chum's brought."

> "Diddle-diddle-damkin, my son John
> Went to bed with a topsail on."

"Your spare rick-cover. —— it, the kid seems to have brought a poop-awning; how in hell does he expect to lash it?"

I did lash it. I got it into my hammock somehow, and then did, in some sort, get my lasher twined about the package. The lasher seemed absurdly short. I had only end enough for five turns, instead of seven, and between two of the turns, a fold or so of the fatal linen peeped; still, it was lashed. I lowered the heap, twisted in the clues, and prepared to carry it down. Now, no little boy ever carried a hammock easily at first. I had carried mine with difficulty the night before, when it had been neat, tight and even. Now, it was none of these things; it was an unwieldy, ill-packed bag, much heavier than the night before by a great weight of bed linen. Somehow, I got this bulging bag sometimes under my arm, sometimes on to my shoulder, and began my tottering march with it to the main hatch of the hold. Such an object was not likely to pass unnoticed; I met with mocks and jeers, and as I passed to port an exceedingly foul-mouthed second-class P.O. into whom I bumped shoved me half across the deck, and almost brought me over, telling me that if I didn't look out, he would —— soon make me, etc. But I got my bundle to the hatch, and then, among the curses of those on the hatch into whom my bundle bumped, I got it down to the hold, where I hoped to dump it into a rack and forget about it till the night. The hammock racks were being watched by the Captains of the Hold, who were very important persons. The second captain dealt with me. "What the hell d'you call that thing?" he asked. "That isn't lashed up. Take it back on deck and lash it up properly."

"Please, I've done it as well as I could."

"Take it to hell out of here, and do it a —— lot better.

That thing isn't going into one of my racks, my cock; so, scatter."

Orders are orders, and have to be obeyed. That was a hard moment, followed by much worse moments, for I now had to carry that heavy bag up the hatch, against the current of men coming down with hammocks. I know that it was a hard passage, during which my eyes and guts and other parts were —— by those who knew no better. On reaching the deck, I had again to run the gauntlet of about a third of the port watch, now back from the lavatory, nearly dressed, and ready to send a new chum spinning if a shove could do it, just to teach the filthy little swine that he wasn't yet god almighty. I felt somewhat lost, when I reached my hammock hook, and reslung my hammock to try to get it better. But now, to my joy, there was the god-like H.B. at his chest under the port, sleeking his locks with a hair-brush in each hand.

"Ha, chum," he said kindly. "In trouble with your hammock? You'll never get a lash-up with sheets like yours. Come on, now; let's see."

He put aside his brushes, swiftly cast loose my lashing, and hove out my sheet. "You can *not* use a thing like that in a hammock," he said. "I blame myself for not thinking of it last night. I'll give you a pair of mine till you can get the proper sort; then you can give me a pair and stick to mine."

"That is most awfully kind of you, sir."

"Don't call me sir."

"Please, what am I to call you, sir?"

"H.B., of course."

"Please, H.B., what can I do with my own sheets?"

"Dump them behind chests for the present."

From his own chest, he plucked a pair of sheets, and flipped them open. He helped me to spread my bedding, roll it, and then lash up. All these things he did very swiftly; all things on board were done swiftly, and now there was need for speed, because almost all hammocks were down, and the orlop deck officer was looking pointedly at me with a grim mouth. Dick joined us, and lent a hand. "I came along a little while ago," he said, "but found you gone."

"I was sent back," I explained.

Dick dumped my pile of bed linen behind the line of sea-chests, saying that we should have to see about it, later. "Get your hammock stowed," he said. The Captains of the Hold growled at my slowness, but let me stow my hammock. I was not happy about my hammock. It had been a cause of much unhappiness, and at half-past eight that evening the unhappiness would begin again. Then, tomorrow morning, I thought, I shall have to hunt for a basin again, and have some more parts of me ——. Still, the thought of H.B. was cheering.

But there I was for the moment, washed and stowed, able to brush my hair and finish dressing on the clear deck, down which sea air was blowing. An old and rheumatic sailor was collecting the extinguished lamps.

Going up to the gangway, I saw a cutter being lowered; and longed to be the man who handled the fall at the cleat, or one of the men in the descending boat hanging on to the life-lines.

Dick caught me as I watched, saying, that there was just time before breakfast to show me what I should have to do. I must first get my knife, fork and spoon "with name engraved" and bring them with me. I ran down to my chest, to get these shining cutleries, and as I pulled them out, to gaze at the beautiful engraving, I was at once beset by three big fellows arm-in-arm, who said they were sure I would give some tuck to three poor maintopmen who would be in the morning cutter instead of getting any breakfast. Of course, I could not let my shipmates starve. No British tar did that kind of thing in the books. I gave some tuck, and at once was beset by a horde of other beggars, with or without excuse, but all ravenous, shameless and without (as I thought) manners. My tuck dwindled, and, then, suddenly, there was Dick again, bidding me to shove my cutlery in my pocket and come along. He showed me, first of all, where my mess table was; at present, slung to the beams above its gun port.

It was called No. 1 mess; I was the youngest hand in it; and therefore my place would be at the bottom, next to the ship's side. When the pipe, went, 'To stand by tables,' I was to come there and stand under the table in my place, ready to lift it down. At the order, I was to lift it down, hold it for an instant, and then make sure that a sort of spike underneath it was neatly engaged within an iron socket ready for it. If this were done smartly, all the better. It did not look difficult; and the table was not heavy, but it was at that time at the extreme limit of my stretch.

This was to be but the beginning of my duty. When this had been done, when the table had been placed, I was to be the messman's assistant, whose job it would be "to muster", that is, attend, at the steward's pantry, to collect the tins containing the mess cutlery, bread, butter, jam and marmalade. The steward would give me these: they would all be in order, ready to take. I was to hurry with them to the mess, who could hardly begin breakfast without them.

Unfortunately, the pipe to 'Stand by Tables' blew at this point: some vital instructions were omitted.

I went to the table. With much difficulty, I did manage to unhook my spike and help to engage it in its socket. I had the feeling, so often strong in unhappy workers, that the others were leaving it all to me. As I could only just reach the table the fact was probably the other way. As soon as the table was placed, Red Swab told me to scatter for the pantry, to get the gear.

I ran down the fore hatch to the pantry, which smelt always charmingly of new bread, and from which all men on board at some time or another hoped to ravish some butter (but very, very seldom could). There were the tins for No. 1 mess; I seized them, and started with them up the fore hatch.

Just at the top of this hatch was the entrance to the galley, or ship's kitchen, from which, at that instant, two dozen other mess servants, known as messmen and mugmen, were bringing food and drink. This stream of men checked my progress, and this check gave the enemy a chance.

At the top of the hatch two or three adroit pirates hovered. These with incredible skill and swiftness grabbed at passing butter and cutlery (they preferred butter) and were away like the light. With hawk-like pounces, they got some of both of mine and were in the stream of men and away to their messes before I knew what they were up to. Nobody had warned me that shipmates could be so wicked; and all laden as I was, hurrying to the waiting mess, not knowing one man in forty of the crew, how could I pursue?

It was my first meal at a mess; I had so often looked forward to it, as a thing of romance, with Tom Bowline on one side, Ben Brace on the other, and old Bill Cutlass calling me "messmate", and occasionally singing "Yo ho". Well, in life the unexpected deals a shock or two to dreams; it did here. When I unloaded my tins at the mess, it was seen at once, by all, that some of the butter and the cutlery had gone. I explained that they had been bagged as I reached the top of the hatch.

"Why did you let them be bagged? Why didn't you look out? Why didn't you stop them? Well, you're not going to have any butter. And hand over your knife, fork and spoon, to make up for those you've lost."

I did as I was bid, feeling somewhat harshly treated;
I had never before been a messman's assistant and had
not been warned of the dangers. I was made to feel that
I was in disgrace, and this although I was already a kind
of pariah, rightly at the bottom of the mess in the place
of ignominy. I was the "youngest hand", not only in the
mess, but in the ship. In the mess, I was served last, or
rather helped myself to the leavings. I found, too, that
my messmates, although only a fortnight senior to myself, were very sure that they were my superiors. I was a
filthy new chum; they were old hands. As I had reduced
the mess cutlery, I had to wait till my elders had finished
with my fork, when I had to use it, to cut my bread and
spread my jam. This was my beautiful, bright fork,
"with name engraved". They said, that I should probably never see my knife, fork and spoon again. All were
washed, after meals, in a communal pot, and sorted out,
thirteen of each kind, to a mess tin, by the galley swabs,
who never bothered about the names. I did come upon
my knife and spoon again, about a year later, but that
was my only meal with my fork.

My messmates, after rude remarks about my incom-
petence and unpleasant appearance, not without some
shrewd thrusts at my sheets, opened general conversation, in which I could join from time to time. Red Swab
sat at the head of the mess upon a stool; we sat upon
forms, six to a side. Naturally, men in a mess talked
most to their near neighbours; and those nearest to me
seemed to be the ones who disliked me most. I could not

see where H.B. was messing. I asked one of the men opposite me in the mess: "Why does H.B. sleep with the focslemen?"

The man very crushingly answered: "Because he chooses."

A good-looking lad, higher up the mess, said: "Because he has his chest at the port, there, so that he can always read; and of course he slings near his chest."

Dick, ever kind and helpful, said: "He can sling just where he likes; he'll only be here a few weeks. He may be ordered abroad almost any day."

The talk ran upon H.B. for a minute. All agreed that he was a most awfully good sort of chap; quite the cleverest man aboard; a jolly good seaman; and excellent at everything he took up; a wonderful swimmer, too; as well as very smart, very good-looking, and liked by everybody. It smote me to the heart to hear that his orders might come so soon. I had known him for about an hour, at most, and in that hour he had shown himself an admirable friend.

"Ah," I thought to myself, "if only I could be in his mess."

Being near the port, I had a good view of the River and its shipping. This was so wonderful to me, that I forgot my worries, till a man asked me what I was staring at? I said: "The River." He said I had better think of my duty, and how not to lose the mess's butter another time. Alas, that thought was not far from me, nor the other thought, how I was to hook the table to the beams when breakfast ended. The thought added, that at every meal the table would bring the same problem, just as every night would bring the same hammock. My heart was still young enough to bounce up after coming down. The River was exquisitely new and beautiful, the most interesting thing I had ever seen. The fact that I was in a ship, in a mess, on a gun deck, one of a ship's company, was overwhelming.

The scene, besides being new, was very beautiful. The deck was well-lighted, and spotless. I had read of decks "white as a hound's tooth"; here I was on such a deck; it was a faultless deck, with wonderful caulking in the seams. This deck was now set with messes in full clatter and clamour; strange faces were in each mess, strange things were everywhere. I did not want food; I was much too excited. I noticed, however, that the food was very good, barring the shortage of butter. A man from the upper part of the mess called out to me that there was a mess club, if I would like to join it. The cost would be tiny every week, and in return we should have sauces, potted meats, pickles, etc., on days when the ship's allowance seemed to indicate something. This seemed a friendly and a sensible arrangement; my moralist opposite said he hoped I would guard the club's goods better than I did the butter.

I kept looking about me, wondering what things were for. Why were those big white rings over the gun ports? Why were they so oddly flexed? What were the big ring-bolts in the deck for? Why were the hatchways guarded with those big rims? What were those things like cut off masts just forward of the mainmast? What were those dish-like depressions in the hatchway rims; and what were the canvas rolls on the beams? The folded desks stowed at the ship's sides were plainly desks for school. "They will be pulled out and set for school presently," someone told me. "Those rolls on the beams are screens, which are let down, to separate class from class."

As the moralist opposite disliked me, he kept asking me: "What I was staring at?" I always said that I was looking at what there was to see; he always retorted, that it was a pity I didn't look out for the mess's butter. In this sentiment, he had the support of the mess; I resolved, that I would die in the defence of the butter next time; either that, or put it somehow inside my tunic or next my skin or something.

A fierce-looking man in the middle of the mess, who had had some butter, and need not have been so crusty, asked me, if I knew any knots. I had heard that this man had been at sea, and judged, from his contempt of us, that this was so.

"What knots do you know?" he asked me. I said, that I could tie a bowline and a reef knot. "Let's see you make a bowline," he said. He had some spun yarn upon him; he handed it over to me. I made my bowline, unmistakably a bowline; I was pleased with it, but he only mocked. "That's a soft way of making a bowline," he said. "Lord, what a way to make a bowline. You'll have to forget that way." He held me up to the mockery of the mess. "Did you see the way he made a bowline? A soft way."

During the meal, a man visited Red Swab on business of some sort. I noticed, that on drawing near he asked: "Can I come in the mess, please?" I asked a man why he did this. The moralist opposite asked me, if I did not know yet, that we all had to ask leave to come into or leave a mess? I did not know, and was told, that I had better soon learn "instead of staring so".

Thinking over that first meal at a mess, I understand how revolting a new face can be. Here was I, an appalling new chum flung down opposite a moralist whose finer feelings had all been outraged by the loss of his butter. He had looked for a proper sense of my iniquity, and had instead seen me light-heartedly staring all over the deck, as though butter came in by the eye. I had looked, it may be, for a messmate's welcome, and had instead found a glare from a butterless gorgon. Even when he had butter (as I found later) he had a face like a coastguard station, and he had a way of eating and drinking. He was a fine fellow, though; we became good friends later; he did very well at sea, and died, in command, many years ago.

In one of the mess tins brought up by me there had been a cloth. This my messmates called "the clout" or "the mess clout". I noticed, that as the meal drew to a close those with any cutlery wiped their (whatever the pirates had left them) on the clout, and pitched the wiped things back into the tin. Men who had finished eating asked: "Clout down the mess, please," and had the clout flung to them.

As ever at this stage of a meal, neat pellets of moulded bread, or bony bits of crust, began to flit from nowhere into the new chums' messes. Some of these were thrown by hand, some jerked from spoons, some catapulted from rubber bands stretched on thumb and forefinger. These last stung, if they caught the ear or the face. The Officer of the deck seemed to wait for these pellets as a sign that the meal was done. He said: "Clear up."

"Up you get, assistant," the moralist said, "now you can stop staring, perhaps." The messman collected all plates, the mugman, all mugs, the assistant, everything else. We did not wash these things; that was done for us, elsewhere. When the tables were cleared and swept, the forms were stowed, the bell was struck, Grace said by a senior P.O. and the awful moment came to stow the table. This was an instant of anguish to me, and like many instants of anguish, not so bad as the dread of it. The table was heavy to my unused arms, and the beams high up to my littleness; still, I got my spike into its catch.

Many years later, being on board, I asked to do the same thing; it was easy enough, then. It was a narrow ship's mess table, made of a good wood which washed to a pleasant whiteness; it was bound at the edges with what looked like galvanised iron, and had swing-legs of the same. In some god-less messes the wicked used to dig out splinters with their forks from the woodwork, and of these splinters made toothpicks.

As we stood in our places, after stowing the tables, the Officer of the day gave his morning orders. "The morning cutters will man the cutter. The starboard main will coal the launch. The dinghy's crew will lower their boat. Clear up decks. Dismiss."

Dick turned upon us. "Get down to the lower deck, the lot of you," he said. Dick was in charge of us that morning, for Red Swab was stroking the morning cutter, then a newly-picked crew. Later, I think they shifted him to one of the midship oars, where his weight would tell more; for he was a big man.

In the first fortnight of every term two cutter's crews were picked from the best oars of the ship. These two crews were called the morning and evening cutters. It was a great privilege to be in either crew, and the first runs of the new crews were watched by a ship's company of men passionately fond of rowing. Seeing a throng of men pressing into the gangway and ports to see the cutter shove off, I followed. I went into the gangway, saw the launch alongside, waiting to be coaled, and the cutter alongside the launch, already manned; the crew in shirt-sleeves, with their oars tossed, and Red Swab looking very happy. Then the lower deck officer saw me, and routed me out of it. "Out of this gangway, you, chum; you've no business here."

"Come on," Dick said, "you're a sweeper this week. Come and get your broom." He showed me where the

brooms were racked; I took one, and joined three other
sweepers in sweeping parts of our side of the lower deck.
The deck was busy with the morning work; the
dinghies were lowering their boat; the starboard main
were at a whip by the fore hatch rushing coal bags up
from the coal hole, with a good deal of noise, and then
charging with the bags, at full speed, to the launch below the gangway. The fury of their zeal was a new thing
to me. I did not then know that the starboard main was
the smart top of that time, and that these men were
showing that they could coal the launch in record time,
though their best hands were off in the cutter. Some Instructors, stewards, mail men and others went off in the
cutter. Dick stopped our sweeping at the line of the
forehatch. "Leave this part, till they've done coaling,"
he said. "Lay aft, and sweep the quarterdeck."

This was then a dark piece of deck, having cabins on
both sides. On the outer walls of the cabins, screened by
brass rails and plate glass, were the Prize Boards of deep
blue, on which the names of all prize winners were
printed in gold. I came to know many of these boards
by heart; in some years outstanding men had won many
prizes apiece. I used to wonder what had become of
these wonders; and what sort of chaps they had been. I
have met some of them since then; I startled two of
them by telling them of their old successes. At the forward end of the Prize Boards was the quarterdeck
proper; at least, one of the sweepers told me that it was.
So this was a quarterdeck. "This is where you'll soon

stand, if you get into trouble," my fellows said. "Standing on the quarterdeck" corresponded to the Marryat punishment "mast-heading". Well, I did stand there, in time; I knew no man who didn't, sooner or later; some poor wretches spent weeks there.

I had never before swept with a broom; and I enjoyed the early parts of the sweep, but when the maintop had finished coaling we four sweepers had to sweep all the coal dust and bits of coal which their zeal had spilled. Brooms had to be passed over the near-by paintwork, and along, and under, the chain cable, for coal dust had settled there. It had to be very thoroughly done, too; Dick had an eye like a hawk. That part of the deck, moreover, was a main throughfare of the ship, and our broadest deck; a lot of space had to be swept. When it was done, my fellows said, that as I was the youngest hand, I must now fetch the dustpan and stow the dirt, by taking it down the gangway and pouring it into the River.

This seemed easy enough, till the lower deck officer icily said to me: "Now that you've spilled all that filthy coal dust down my gangway, you'll just fetch your broom and sweep the whole stair down."

I had been told that the rule of the ship was: "Obey first, growl afterwards." A wit had added that the real rule was: "Obey first; and if you growl afterwards you'll have to do it again ten times." This seemed nearer the truth, so I swept the gangway stairs as bidden, wondering how I could keep dust from blowing on to them another time; they had fretted brass treads, into which coal dust blew and stuck. I was now less happy with my broom. My fellows had told me that we had to sweep the whole deck eight times a day, and that even then it wouldn't look too good. We should be sweepers for a week; then another four would sweep, but our turn would come once or twice more before the holidays.

"I want you," Dick said. "Come on here. These two staunchions will be your job; you'll have to polish them each morning. Have you ever polished staunchions?"

"No; never."

"You do it with this fine sand-paper, which we keep here; and remember, sand-paper can be used until it rubs to dust. Heave round on these staunchions, now, and let's see how bright you can make them."

The two staunchions were the steel staunchions just forward of the after-capstan. To clean them, I had to stand on the grating; it was at this point that I began to understand what a miracle the ship was. I was standing on a grating, a work of art, such as I had never seen. How had men cut and fitted hard white wood so exquisitely into this lattice? The coamings round the grating, supporting it, were other miracles; but nothing to the astounding deck. I began now to appreciate the deck: it was something which I could never have imagined. It was of a darkish wood; and all the deck was laid with it; even I could judge that a hundred very big trees, at least, must have died to yield its timber. It was of a hardness which I had never thought wood could have; it was more like dark glass than wood. How had men cut it, shaped it, bent it and secured it?

"Looking at the deck?" Dick said. "It's African oak. When it is wet tomorrow, you can take off your shoes and stockings and slide on it barefoot; it is quite impossible for you to get a splinter. Now, heave round."

He had given me a tin containing sand-paper, rags, and a sort of brick; I took some sand-paper and began upon a staunchion. Round the brow and the ankle of this steel shaft were plaits of dark cord, which seemed to have neither beginning nor end; certainly, I had joined a miraculous world. Then, I was within reach of a capstan; an enormous capstan, with sockets for the bars, and fittings which I did not understand. I did not see any bars for it, and I could not make out how we should go yo-ho-ing round it if any bars were fitted; still, what did that matter? it was a capstan, and within reach.

I worked at my staunchion, which did not become much brighter, because I was so thrilled by all that I saw. Close to me, to port, was a real, modern, breech-loading cannon, with traversing channels, side tackles and the rest of it. H.B. was there, in charge of a team, making it to shine like the stars; it all shone, with steeliness, brassiness and blackness.

"Come. Come. That isn't the way to make a staunchion bright," Dick said. "Just watch me for a moment."

Certainly, his method made the steel like silver; I found that I could do it, and that it was great fun. "Those will be your staunchions, every morning," Dick said. "Now get a bucket from the manger, fill it at the gangway, and don't fall in and drown yourself." I did his bidding, and learned a good deal by it; that buckets can have rope handles with fascinating knots on them, that a tide may fill a bucket with a surprising rush, and that when full of water it can seem very heavy to a little boy's arms, and that what slops over will drown his shoes.

Then came another astounding play. While I fetched the water, Dick had armed two of my focsle with what looked like the back hair of the coarser kind of mermaid. He said, that we had to swab down, where the coal-bags had marked the deck. I knew from this, that the back hair things were swabs. I had read of swabs. In the books, seamen spoke of incompetent officers as swabs, sometimes as lubberly swabs; so these were swabs. Dick took my bucket, scooped out the water with a hand, and directed the swabbers to flop the wetness with the back hair, and lo, the darkness where bags had dragged went out under the flop. Very soon, I was sent for another bucket of water; and then directed to give one of the swabbers a spell-oh, or relief, by taking his swab.

I did not like this so well, but worse followed. The swabbers turned on me at the end of the work, saying: "You're the youngest hand. You'll take the swabs down the gangway, rinse them, wring them dry, and stow them in the manger."

Dick confirmed this order; it was the youngest hand's job; and I was the youngest hand beyond all doubt.

The lower deck officer had had his eye on me for some time. "None of your drips down this gangway," he said. "Hold the wet ends of those swabs up, so that they don't drip on the stairs."

I did this, and very cold, wet and heavy the two swabs were. However, when I was at the foot of the steps, the officer's messenger, who had been a new chum himself the term before, gave me friendly advice. "Don't rinse the swabs," he said, "all the wet you get on to them you'll have to wring out of them; and it's the coldest job going. Just damp the tips."

I was indignant. What, disobey an order, during my first working day? Try to deceive the kind Dick? Not I. I soused the swabs well and hung them, to wring them.

Worldly wisdom, such as the messenger had advised, was known on board as "being lairy". Superior conduct, such as mine, was known as "being ambi". My heart glowed, that I had made the choice.

The swabs were sopped, and I had to wring them dry. I took them lock by lock, and all the water I wrung from one lock seemed to go back into the swab, while my hands grew colder and colder, and the lower deck officer asked how much longer I was going to be, slopping puddles on his grating?

Then, a brilliant thought struck me; the water, so cold to wring out, might be trodden out. I laid the swabs flat and trod upon them, and by some miracle was not seen and jumped upon. I trod them, I will not say dry, but drier than they had been, and in this state bore them to the manger. The manger still stands. I always go to see it when I go aboard. It is a stout barrier, built across the fore lower deck, designed, originally, to keep water from washing aft from the hawse holes whenever the ship was in soundings. In the past, it had been a place of privilege: the "Yeomen of the Manger" had slung their hammocks there; and being only four (or perhaps, six) had had more space for their hammocks than most of the ship's company.

To a little boy, it was a barrier. It had to be climbed, for the proper stowage of the gear, and though climbing came easily to me, this was a special sort of climbing, in which I had to keep my uniform clean, and, much more important, the paint upon the manger's face unspotted. In my vivid memories of those days the manger stands up as a barrier; when I see it now, I feel that it must have been cut two feet. Remember, reader, that I had to climb it with two damp swabs, each nearly as long as myself, and weighing, as it seemed to me, a young ton, and that these had to be kept off the paint.

When I had stowed the swabs, there was a rush and hurrahing on the deck, as a gang of men charged from the gangway to the steward's pantry. The morning cutter had returned, bringing the relief staff, the mails and the bread. The bread came daily in a big canvas-covered basket, exactly like those used by travelling theatrical companies for clothes and properties. It was this basket which now advanced. It dispelled about itself the delightful smell of very hot new bread. Its coming attracted many other men besides the cutter's crew; about twenty gathered in a pack at the pantry door, and I saw that certain of them were trying to thrust their hands under the basket lid to steal the bread. This the steward checked, saying, that if they so much as stole one piece, he would report them, and not give the cutter's crew any. As it was hard to steal bread from under the lid (nobody ever got more than a taste that way) and as the cutters were in a hurry, having to haul their boat out, the thieves were checked; the basket was unlocked; and in such a way, that the lid stood up as a shield. The steward and a couple of trusties rapidly emptied the basket, putting the loaves on the shelves. As soon as it was cleared, it was run to one side, and the steward, who had much natural authority, and the eyes of a hawk, guarding his wealth of hot bread, jam, and prepared butter pats from pirates, each as clever as a cat, took one hot loaf, and gave it to the chief trusty. This man was at once beset, by all the mob, but having some strength, he broke it into bits and doled it to the cutter's crew. Instantly, each holder of a piece of hot bread, was beset by a gang of beggars, with cries of "Your spare sodduk", and in another instant, the hot dough was swallowed and gone. I asked a focsleman what sodduk was; he looked at me with much contempt, and said: "Why; bread."

One of the gang who had been trying for hot bread was the man who had told me to haul at 'Light-to' the night before, and had caused me a cruel fall; he did not seem to bear me any grudge, for he said: "Can you swim?"

"Yes."

"Well, I'll give you a good tip. Say you can't swim; and pretend you can't. All new chums go to the Baths in Liverpool every morning until they can swim, and they get off school and everything else. You needn't do a stroke the whole term if you're half smart."

This was the voice of the tempter; I could only say: "But I can swim."

"Oh, of course; if you like to be an ass . . ."

Dick caught me here. "You wanted to order some hammock sheets?" he said. "Come on, into the office here. The Gunner will do that for you."

The Gunner said that that could be easily arranged, and did it: sheets troubled me no more.

"Now," Dick said, "that's 'Hands. Dress'. Come on down, now, and dress for Divisions."

On going down, I found the orlop deck already crowded with hands dressing, that is, they were blacking their shoes, each at his chest, while some brushed tunics, or stood while a friend brushed them. I had never blacked my shoes, but there, in my till, were some brushes for the purpose, and a bright tin full of very good blacking. Dick told me that one of my brushes was a blacker, the other a polisher, and that which ever I used for either purpose should be kept for that. I know, that I made an unusual choice, but in the shining of the shoes the man counts, not the brushes. Now my shoes were new, and new shoes never polished well; they were also wet through from the buckets and the swabs, and wet shoes always look rather dull. Dick looked doubtfully at them, and said that new shoes were always hard to polish. My tunic was new, and looked well; after a touch with a clothes-brush, Dick said that I should pass all right. I was made to feel, that the inspection was strict. Dick was in earnest, and the men near me were taking pains, and posing before their neighbours, with odd questions. "How are my dead-eyes for square?" or "Am I all square by the lifts and braces?" or "Am I correct magnetic?" The answers were equally strange. "Your laniards are hanging down" or "Well, since you ask, you look like the wrath of God".

The greater number were really taking pains; not all, however. I noticed that some men were not polishing their shoes, but using a tiny smear of vaseline to give a fictitious brightness to the surface; and some, waiting till the very last instant, were about to moisten their toe-caps with water, for a wet shoe may sometimes shine so as to deceive. Later, I knew that this trick was silly; for the wetted surface swiftly dulls, and then looks most slovenly. Almost at once, a rather longer whistle blew, and somebody shouted something. "That's Divisions," Dick said, "buck up, now, to the main deck to fall in."

When we had fallen in, I was in the front row, and had a good view of the port watch; some looked smart, some tough, some dangerous; but I was already beginning to take sides, and to think that they were not so smart, so tough, nor as dangerous as my own fine watch mates. Presently, we were called to attention, told to dress up to deck seams; then the Gunner slowly inspected us, front and back. He stopped at me, and told me, that I must get my shoes brighter than that. He called Red Swab, showed him my shoes, and said that my shoes were not bright. Red Swab said that I had just come aboard, that my shoes were new, and that new shoes never took a polish. The Gunner shook his head, and glowered at me. "You get your captain, here," he said, "to give you a lesson in shoe cleaning. He's a good hand at it. Look at his shoes. Don't come to Divisions with shoes like that again." He passed on, but my neighbour whispered that I needn't pay any attention, since the Gunner wouldn't hurt a fly.

When both watches had been inspected and the slovenly admonished, the mail master was told to serve out letters. He did this, by pitching letters and parcels one by one on to the after-grating, calling out the name upon each. When this had been done it was about 8.40; the order came to place forms for prayers. The mizen-topmen, going two men to each form, placed all the forms, and the chairs for Officers and Masters in a minute; they could rig the more elaborate church on Sundays in a minute and a half. We were marched to our places, the bell struck, the Captain and Chaplain entered, and Prayers began. As before, the new chums thought more of possible pins than of praying; but the service was brief. The Captain received some reports after the service; on special occasions he sometimes spoke to us (usually with displeasure), and then dismissed us. On this, my first morning, he dismissed us. Dick told me that now it was school, almost nine o'clock, and that now the main deck would be rigged for school, and that I had a minute in which to go to my chest to get my pen and ink. Alas, I had neither, and asked, in some wonder, if these were not supplied. "Which Class are you in?" Dick asked. I said I didn't know. "Ah," he said, "of course. You haven't been examined yet. You'll probably be in the Fourth. They'll give you a slate, there. Bring up your Navigation Tables." It sounded very grand, to be in the fourth class already, and to bring up my Navigation Tables, but what was this, about being given a slate? But I saw at once that men were hurrying. The main deck was being turned into a school. The maintopmen were letting down the canvas screens, and rigging the lines of desks, bringing out black-boards and setting forms. The mizentopmen could rig forms in one minute. The maintopmen could rig school in two; their smartness at the work had to be seen to be believed. As I went below, men were already streaming up, carrying small piles of books, and safety ink-pots, wrongly supposed to be unspillable. These men, as they hurried up to school, called "Gangway, gangway," to warn men from their path; two or three of them swore at me for not giving gangway enough. One of them, a fair-haired young man, with a terrible countenance, said he would knock my something eyes out. I had run into him that early morning and would fain have avoided him. He looked like a pirate who had swum in blood from his cradle; he continued about my eyes for some time.

Learning from this encounter to walk more circumspectly, I reached my chest, took my Navigation and Tables, two small folio volumes, strongly bound, and went again to the main deck, which had now been changed into schoolrooms, with desks, forms and blackboards. A canvas screen athwart-ships, just abaft the mainmast, parted the senior from the junior classes.

As I came up, looking rather lost, the man called Frog's-Guts caught me. "Here, you," he said, "nip into the carpenter there, and ask for the key of the keelson." Well, I knew about this. Instantly, however, some strangers came on me, with: "Hey, chum . . . What's your name?" I told them.

"That's the name," they said. "You're the chap. The Skipper's waiting for you in his office, just inside the Quarters door there. He wants to know why you haven't been examined. He's furious with you for not reporting."

"I didn't know I had to report."

"That won't save you. Have you been examined?"

"No."

"Well, you'd better cut. He'll skin you alive for keeping him waiting. I never saw him so angry."

The news was shocking enough to be true . . . and yet . . . Dick would have told me, if I had had to report.

The entrance of the Masters at this point made my advisers scatter to their places, but to the last, they persisted, pointing aft, in the direction of the Quarters. A master with a kindly face saw me lost between the three junior classes, and finding that I had not been examined, sent me to the Chaplain, who had charge of the Second Class. The examination was brief, but sufficient.

Chaplain: "What French have you done?"

I named two books, some of which I had translated; also two grammars, some of which I had read. He had not heard of the books, but knew the grammars.

Chaplain: "What Navigation have you done?"

Myself: "None, sir."

Chaplain: "Or Nautical Astronomy?"

Myself: "None, sir."

Chaplain: "You will be in the Fourth Class, under Mr. Foxley, just across the deck there. You can go to him."

I thanked him, and walked over to Mr. Foxley, who was the kindly man who had spoken to me. He had expected me, evidently, for there was a place for me, into which I went; somebody in the class handed me a slate and a slate pencil, both of which seemed to me humiliations. I was then able to look about me and take stock of another strangeness in this extraordinary life.

There was no doubt that the Fourth Class was the lowest class in the ship. It was manned almost wholly by new chums, but one or two old hands, physically incapable of learning anything, were somehow stuck there as unfit for anything else. We sat in the main, not wholly, in two tight rows of desks, between the Instructors' cabin, which we faced, and the screened central space, looking down into the hold, to where the ship's engines had once been. A lowered canvas screen shut us from sight of the galley, but we could at times hear the whistles, songs and conversations of the cooks and stewards at work there. Looking aft, we had a good view of the Third Class, with its black-board and Master; turning round, we could see something of the Second Class, under the Chaplain. Well, though we in the Fourth were low in the ship, we were not downhearted. By some excess in our numbers, we were not all facing the Master; a row of desks was arranged en potence from us, parallel with the midship coaming of the great open space. These men diverted the Master's attention half the time; I found at once, that a good deal of conversation could be quietly carried on. My neighbours were not a winning couple at first sight. My right-hand neighbour was the man who had told me to haul at the order 'Light-to', the night before, causing me a painful fall. I asked: "If we were marked, and placed according to our work in form?" He said: "No. There's nothing of all that. We're shoved up anyhow into another form at the beginning of each term, by new men coming on board." I asked: "If we never did preparation?" He seemed to think it a scholastic subject. "What is that?" he asked. When I explained he told me: "No; of course not."

My left-hand neighbour was a very strange looking fellow, who resembled the description of the villain in my favourite romance. On seeing him, I quoted to myself some words of that romance. "Thou art my enemy;" but in this I soon learned my folly. He was a simple, but very good-natured man, three or four years older than myself, a senior maintopman, brawny and active, but quite incapable of learning anything in any school subject. He could read and write, of course; there his faculties baulked, and though several terms of new chums had brought him close to a remove, he had not yet been shoved up into a higher form. He made little or no effort to learn anything from the Master; he was both uninterested and incapable. He had with him always in school a piece of spun-yarn or other line, with which he practised knots and splices. He was a good practical seaman; and as I had never seen such things made, I watched his deftness with wonder; and learned; and in good time learned, that such talent was treasúred on board. With a bit of spun-yarn or other line, he got through the first two lessons of the morning without great unhappiness. He told me, that our Master "took us" in all school classes, teaching Navigation of a primitive kind, the Day's Work and similar easy problems, Arithmetic, Algebra, English, History, Geography and Scripture. French he said was only done once a week, in the forward hospital; he said it was great fun. Presently I found that it was reckoned so, by the pupils of the unhappy French gentleman who came aboard to teach us.

The slate seemed to me to be a going back to childhood. What had sailors to do with slates? My neighbour said that it was to save the deck from spilled ink; that we, being mostly new chums, were not supposed to be safe with ink-pots, and therefore had to use slates. He thought this a wise rule. He was a maintopman, responsible for that bit of the deck, which was the approach to the galley and therefore very much used and difficult to keep white. I did not then know the pride of the maintopmen in their deck, nor the standard they maintained.

I had been but a very few minutes in the class, when the Messenger brought word that the Captain wanted me in the Sick Bay. My heart went down to the soles of my wet shoes. He *had* wished to see me, after all, then; and I had defied his orders. One of my classmen said: "Another time you'll go when he orders you. You'll get a month's jumper; pretty good for your first day. Go on

your knees to him; then he may let you off with a
week."

In a cold sweat of terror I went hurriedly to the Sick
Bay, and quakingly knocked and entered. There was
the Captain, with a Doctor, the Nurse and a few
patients. I saw a light airy room, with big bottles
of remedies; black-draught, cough-mixture, gargle,
arnica, etc.; perhaps half a dozen beds and two paintings of frigates at anchor in the Sloyne. The Captain
looked appalling. I supposed that he would now hang
me at a yardarm.

I was told to strip tunic and shirt. It was less terrible
than I had feared. All new chums had to be vaccinated
before coming aboard; the examination was only to see
that I had been vaccinated, and that the scars permitted
me to do the ship's work. As my scars were long since
healed, I was at once dismissed, and went forth knowing
that the Captain saw everything, and that when he
thundered the son of Adam would be but as dust.

On my way out, I was stopped by the Gunner, who
asked: "Can you swim?"

I said that I could, but on being pressed, could not
say how far I could swim, never having tried.

"You must join the bathing party there, then," he
said. "You need not take any things with you; they'll
give you those at the Baths."

I joined the bathing party, of some thirty new chums,
including my neighbour from the fourth class. We
went down into the steam launch's roomy cabin, and

away to Liverpool. My bathing party urged me to pretend that I couldn't swim. "We can all swim," they said, "but we get out of morning school every day. Don't be a silly ass. If you just pretend a little, you'll be able to do the same."

As we drew near to Liverpool, I went on deck, to see the sights. I looked to port, at the Woodside pier, for I knew that just there was the station which led back home. Above it were the lofty masts and square white yards which had caught my eye in that long distant century, the day before. Somehow they seemed more splendid than any other masts; I could not get them out of my head; I haven't got them out of my head yet.

At the Baths, in spite of their exquisite excellence, to be described later, and in spite of adjurations, not to be an ass, I plunged in and swam straight across, and was told that I need not join another bathing party; I could swim. All the way back to the ship, I was told that I was an ass; an ambi ass.

Morning school was not quite over when we returned aboard; we had the tail-end of a lesson in Navigation. My neighbour, the old maintopman, told me that he always did seamanship of some sort until the mid-morning break, and that after break, he passed the time in eating. During break, it seemed, soup, coffee and hard tack could be had by anyone who felt at all faint; he always laid in a store of food to last him till lunch. I well remember, that that morning, just after my return, our Master turned to this man, and said:

". . . Stop eating hard tack."

With a sense of wrong, of being falsely accused, my neighbour said: "Please, sir, I'm not eating hard tack."

"Well," the Master said, "stop eating whatever you *are* eating. What are you eating?"

"Soft tack, sir."

Now Mr. Foxley turned to me, and explained that I was to find a ship's position by Dead Reckoning, that is, I was to work a Day's Work by Inspection.

I was shown how to draw on my slate a fascinating image of a page of a ship's log, with a note of my departure, my courses, distances and leeways. Next, I had to look up certain traverse tables, in *Rapers' Tables*, which had nothing to do with food or the mess, and then, if I made no mistake, there was my ship's position. All this, I thought, was potty. I did it, and was told that I was right. Well, I thought, if this is navigation, surely, I have found my calling. To the right of my log, was a Remarks Column. Mr. Foxley told me that I should enter in this what had seemed unusual in the day, what derelicts I had passed, what steps I had taken to avoid drifting ice, etc., what ships I had spoken, and the nature of our signals. Finding that I showed interest in the problem, he told me that I must not trust to Dead Reckonings, but take Sights whenever I had any chance of taking them. He said: "Presently you will hear about variable currents, tides, compass deviations and the uncertainty of distances run. A sight is called 'a fix'; a day's work is called 'a fudge'."

The tail-end of morning school was usually slacker than the earlier hours; the attentions of the young had flagged, and men talked more. This led, in the end, to some of them being told to stand upon the form. This did not matter to the small man, but if you were tall, your head bumped into the beams, and you had to stoop to avoid them. The very tall looked very odd as they stood on the form and bent to write at the desk. The Captain visited each class once every morning, varying his times according to his fancy. He did not add to the punishment of those standing on the forms, but his visit was dreaded by them. He had a way of fixing the culprit with a grim eye, which struck terror into the boldest. Then, his: "Well, sir, and what has this offender been doing?" and then, his devastating question to the guilty: "What do you mean by this, sir?" He came round the classes on that first morning of mine. Suddenly the mutter or wash of conversation being carried on by at least fifty boys under their breaths in the five classes died away; and my neighbours muttered: "The Skipper," and at once bent to their books as though learning was the one thing they sought from life. The awful stillness grew as he came nearer; then, there he was, spotless, smart, well set-up, a very splendid figure, standing talking to our Master, always saying something interesting or to the point, rather like Zeus, sometimes not thinking us worth the lightning we deserved. He would stay for perhaps a dreadful minute, filling both guilty and virtuous with unease,

wondering what he had done wrong, and quaking lest
Zeus should suddenly tell him. To most of us he was
a first acquaintance with sea discipline; he was a ship's
Captain, an absolute authority.

When school ceased, I put my books and slate in my
chest, took my broom, and swept my deck again, while
maintopmen rolled up the canvas screens, and stowed
the desks and forms. In a few minutes, we had to stand
by our tables for dinner; and this moment I dreaded
still, being not tall enough to reach the table easily.
After our table was placed, I had to run for the knives
and forks tin; and this time guarded it against the
pirates. The pipe was blowing the long and cheery
'Pipe to dinner', which must once have sent eight hundred hungry men to their meal on board that same
ship. Though I was not hungry, being still excited, and
perhaps not quite unrefreshed with tuck, I was interested to see how we should be fed. I had been cheered
at breakfast, dinner was much more cheering; our
caterer served us exceedingly well; and the mess club
filled the lacks. We were not given bread at dinner.
Those who wanted it had to save some at breakfast or
collect hard tack in the break. We were not given water
to drink at dinner. If we wished for a drink at the meal,
we had to go to a water tank by the main mast, and
drink there from the communal mug secured to the
tap. After the meal, when the tables had been stowed,
we were ordered to clear up decks, and dress in jumpers, for Sail Drill.

Sail Drill, the words would thrill any boy.

I had been busily engaged all day, and had not been aloft. I knew that no new chums were allowed aloft in Sail Drill; they worked on deck, while the older hands had the fun and the glory. Still, I should see sails; I should sing yo-ho no doubt; and perhaps hear the Captain shouting through the speaking-trumpet: "Give her the main topmast studding-sail. Lively now, the starboard focsle."

After sweeping, I went to my chest with thrilling heart. Dick pulled out the coarse blue serge coat with black buttons, which he said was the jumper. Having put this on, I waited till the pipe summoned us up to drill. We fell in to our divisions; the Chief appeared, to take the exercise.

"Now for it," I thought. It was not so. Red Swab said that it would fall to us first, to fetch the sails up from the sail locker down in the hold.

In another minute, we were racing down into the hold, to that musty, bilge-reeking inclined plane down which I had run for my hammock the night before. Here, a Captain of the Hold, with a lantern, showed us a heap which he said was the maintopsail. There was a strong smell of tar and a sour smell of canvas, as well as the other smells. I understood nothing of what was happening, except that we had been ordered to work the main mast. Red Swab cried: "Claw on to this, now. Get it on to your shoulders. Heave it out, now. Buck your stumps, and up with it." He was an old maintopman, of course, and meant his old mates of the main to have their sail bent before their rivals, the fore. We clawed on to the topsail; of course, half of us were treading on it, and at the same time, the port focsle was trying to claw on to the foretopsail, on which the other half were treading. There was hardly any light, and none of us chums knew what we were doing; but Red Swab and Dick together hove; and we were not going to be beaten by the other watch; not if our deaths could stop it, so up we hove the roll; and at once decided that if this were a sail, it was not in the least like the white wing to which it has been likened in song. Having it more or less on our shoulders, we barged out of the locker into light, and tottered towards the hatch. The sail was old, but a big, deep naval single topsail, even if old, can be heavy, and exceedingly knobby. We went stumbling along, urged on by Red Swab, and cursed by men in front and behind us, who said that we were leaving it all to them. Iron things, called cringles, seemed to come exactly opposite every bone in my upper body, and to grind right in. Of course, I was carrying the whole topsail; no one else was carrying any. I did it, too. I got that topsail to the upper deck and dumped it down, and thought, now, after all that, I shall be granted a little time to breathe.

In this I was wrong. An Officer was waiting for me. He fixed a grim eye on me, and said: "Watch very carefully what is done, and remember it, for you will have to do it next time yourself." He made us open up the bundle and make it up for bending. I had never seen a sail before, close to. I did not know one part of it from another; yet I remembered what he showed me for years to come.

There came a pipe and a shout: "Fore and maintopmen, stand by to go aloft." At once, there was a rush of the waiting topmen to the chains. I saw a cluster of eager heads above the hammock-nettings, though these were checked by the Officer with: "Now, quietly. Get down below the sheer poles, there." In another second there came another pipe and order. "In the tops. Way aloft," and at once those eager men surged forward, in the race to be first into the tops. I had never before seen smart hands going aloft. Our men were smart. That desperate rush was a sight to see and remember. It is a running up very steep stairs at top speed. The stairs are made of rope; those who take them at speed often miss a step, and the foot drops into a gap and the rope step scrapes the shin, the man below gets a knock and punches the offender; but all these by-plays happen so fast that they are not noticed from the deck. Men went up at such speed that in the Navy, they used to give a moment for breath directly the hands had reached the tops. Such a moment was well deserved, and often much needed; no doubt our own system allowed for it, but Red Swab clouted me with the peak of his cap and told me not to stand gaping there, but tally-on to the gantline; so I, not knowing what a gantline was nor what was meant by tallying-on, but seeing a rope manned, tallied-on to it, and ran the topsail up, so that it was at the yard by the time the men were there. In an instant, as it seemed, the topsails were stretched along and bent; then, they were let fall, so that the wind caught and bellied them; and gazing aloft, I saw the men far aloft on the topgallants cast loose their sails, while all the yardmen scurried in off their yards and the sails wallopped and slatted. The Officer taking the drill called something after something. I never knew what he said, but Red Swab or Dick hurried me to some rope or other, and told me to haul like hell or put my weight on. I always did as I was bid, and sometimes had a fair reward, in seeing what I had done. I know, now, that the sails were sheeted home and hoisted; and looked superb, when set; but that just as they were beginning to send the ship ahead, to ease her moorings a little, an order sent us all to the braces. "Weather topsail braces," came the order. I did not know what they did nor where they were, but I was hurried aft to their cleat; again we hauled; and had hardly finished, before some other devilry had begun; reefs had to come in; I had to hop to the reef tackles. I had some glimpses of wonders aloft, devil-may-care men at the yardarms, with one foot free, astride the yards, handling the ear-rings like the leading seamen they were. Orders were shouted about dog's lugs, and to lay in; and then to me, not to stare aloft but put my weight on the halliards,

We had scarcely got the sail re-hoisted, when more reefs had to come in; then the sails were furled; most of the men came down from aloft; and there came a minute during which ropes were coiled up or down, so as to leave a clear deck.

After this, came spar drill, which was much less interesting to a new chum, but better fun to the trusty hands allowed aloft. These were among the best men on board. They went in couples to the cross-trees; and in a few seconds, the top gallant yards came flying down, to be snatched into the shrouds and lashed there. After them, down came the top gallant masts. I was told to man the tripping line, which I did, thinking it a rather jolly name. We had the spars flat on deck; I saw the main top gallant mast close to, for a moment; then we sent the spars up once more, and re-crossed the yards. Other men now took the places of those aloft, and the drill was repeated. I hauled on the yard ropes and the tripping lines, and ran as I was bidden, but had not the dimmest notion of what my efforts helped to do. A day before, I had been a landsman, now I was one of a crew, very willing but completely puzzled; and wondering whether I should ever remember the different ropes. Under the main mast there seemed to be a lot of ropes; under the fore mast were at least as many more and just as I despaired of learning either, Red Swab hurried me forward, to new puzzles. We were running to rig out, rig in, then rig out again, the flying jibboom, and to hoist, dowse, and re-hoist, a jib, which at last the foretopmen furled. In fact, like the Jovial Huntsman

"I powlert up and down a bit and had a rattling day,
    Look ye there."

At the end of the exercise, it fell to us slaves to coil up or down the running rigging which had been in use. I learned to "light", that is, to pass the rope to the coilers, and in doing this learned what a kink is, and how to deal with it. After this, we were dismissed, to change out of our jumpers and to pass the time till tea.

Coming on deck again, I was met by two mizentopmen, who asked me, if I had been aloft yet? I had to say, No. They asked, would I care to come up with them? I said I would. They said that it was not at all difficult, except going over the futtocks, which they pointed out to me, as iron bars leaning outwards from the mast to the top rim. I should have to lean outwards as I climbed these, they said, with my back downwards, and the certainty of going overboard if I let go. However, they said that if I couldn't manage the futtocks, there was another way. This, I had already heard of, and was determined to die rather than use it, though some had told me that I was the new chum the place had been left for. I looked up at the futtocks, with the thought that in all my climbing, and I had done a good deal, the getting down was a lot worse than going up, but that it would be time to think of getting down when I had been up.

With this, I followed my two guides through a port

(we had no Jacob's Ladders) into the port fore chains, where I slipped to the outboard side of the dead-eyes, marvelling at their size, and the tautness of their laniards. The way up seemed easy, with lots of little rope steps; so up I went, till I was at the futtocks looking down upon the nets spread for me, lest I should fall inboard, at the River spread for me, if I should fall outboard, and at the top rim above me, in case I ever got there. An unknown world of cross-trees and trucks lay beyond it, out of sight. "Don't look down," one of my guides said. I answered, that I had to get used to looking down sooner or later, and had better begin at once. One of my guides said: "Now, if you don't feel you can go over the futtocks, you can go through the lubber's hole, there."

Those who remember the naval top and lubber's holes, will know that in some ways they were even more difficult than the futtocks. I never tried them, as there was a prejudice against them, but I have been told this by those who knew them; my own observation of them confirms this; they were not easy. The futtocks close to looked pretty grim. Looking up from their foot I saw the blank top rim, the arm of the topsail yard, and the giddy top gallant above it. One of my guides said: "Watch me, and do what I do." He laid hold of the iron bars, went swiftly up, half-disappeared, kicked with a friendly leg or so, and then peered over the top rim to call out: "Up you come, now; it's as easy as kiss."

I laid hold of the iron bars and squeezed them pretty

tight. I went up, and put a groping hand over the top
rim for something secure. My guide put my hand on to
something sure; I know not now which, and with a
heave I was over the rim in the top, much surprised, to
find it tenanted by two young men who were lying
prone on its broad surface, invisible from below, enjoying a quiet smoke. Some crevices in the planking of the
top showed that this was a frequented smoking place, as
they held a good many cigarette-butts and matches.
The young men looked at me with some contempt.
To them I was only a new chum, being ambi; they
turned to their delight, and I to mine.

I was, of course, vain of my prowess in getting there,
but this was nothing to the experience of being there.
It was a matchless September afternoon, clear, sunny
and full of colour. The view was superb. The River
stretched up and down for miles. The drying sails in
the ships in dock shone in the sun; the westward front-
ing windows gleamed; ships and lesser craft moved on
their courses; whatever squalor was in that double city
(and there was plenty) was invisible from where I stood.
Close to me, almost at my feet, was the big Cunarder of
the week, certain to sail next day for New York City.
She had lighters alongside, and her wonderful tender,
the *Skirmisher*. A little to westward from her was a
wide bay, then smoky buildings, then a distance full of
mountains, for one looked straight across to Snowdon.
One of my guides pointed out a heap half-submerged
in the bay. "You see the wreck, there," he said. "She was

lying at anchor, when a ship went into her and cut her in two. I was near the gangway when we heard the alarm, and I went in the lifeboat's crew. I wish I hadn't gone. They were all dead when we got there. We could see where they'd been caught asleep, and how they'd tried to get out. The other half of her sank, but the current put that one where she lies."

I looked at the heap with the fascination which youth feels for horror of every kind, and envied my guide his experience. My other guide was not to be outdone. He bade me look up-stream, to another heap ashore on the shingle beyond the New Ferry pier. "You see that?" he asked. "That is all that's left of the *Great Eastern,* once the biggest ship in the world."

I had often heard of that triumph of man. I had once had an image of her, printed upon a handkerchief, a delight to childhood; now I was looking at the ship herself; all that was left of her. "Yes," my guide went on, "she was a wonder in her day. She was built with a double bottom; so that she could not be sunk; and a riveter got riveted in between the two skins; and he knocked and knocked, to call attention; and for years afterwards his ghost used to knock. The crews couldn't stand it; and she was always an unlucky ship. Well, when they opened her up, on the beach, they found his skeleton between the skins, with a hammer tight in his finger-bones, and the head of the hammer all worn away with knocking."

This was too much for my other guide; this was hearsay; he had seen his horrors with his own eyes, and now described them, in words not forgotten. There is a line of Browning:

"The fight must so have seemed in that fell cirque."

I have thought of that crew's death for years.

When I had had a good look round, I looked up, to the white cross-trees above me and the topgallant yard above them. "What d'you think of going up to the cross-trees?" one of the guides asked. "Of course, it's nothing, after the futtocks. You could go alone to the cross-trees. I wouldn't try the truck, the first day." I saw the truck, at the summit of the mast, and felt that perhaps he might be right about it. But I went up to the cross-trees, and getting on to them, stood, holding on to whatever seemed stable. It was a fine blowy perch up there. I felt like a real sailor, so near to a real yard and sail, with the truck only a few feet above me. I had read of a boy standing on a truck. There a truck was for me to stand on, if I felt like it, but somehow I thought I would put it off till I could enjoy it more; and then, standing on a truck is a selfish pleasure; a man needs all the truck to himself; you can't share it with a friend. But I thought of that boy standing on the truck "whence all but he had fled", and of the picture, showing him there, with his father standing aft with a gun, calling: "Jump . . . 'tis your only chance of life."

The cross-trees were of white painted wood; they had not been painted recently and someone had cut his

initials E.R. on them. The letters were well-cut, and
had long weathered; they must have been done years
before. I wondered who E.R. was, and why his were
the only initials. Very few initials were cut in the floor
of the top; one or two, perhaps, but not the hundreds
one would have expected. I remembered, too, that the
school desks were not cut. As I had now seen the cross-
trees, and felt that perhaps if I delayed my guides might
leave me to get down the futtocks by myself, I went
down to the top, and asked why so few names were cut.
"Why," my guides said, "that would be damaging
ship's property; you'd be black-listed for that. Besides,
if a new chum were to do it, he'd have the whole of
both foretops down on him, for insulting the foretops;
and only new chums go aloft. When you are in a top,
and have been a term on board, you'll never come up
here except at sail drill. Why the hell should you;
except to be nearer?" (He meant "nearer heaven.")

As I was a new chum, there for the first time, aloft,
in a top, I could not know the truth of what he said. It
seemed that it was little use supplying two hundred
boys with jack-knives and laniards if there were to be
this prejudice against a little friendly carving. I had
learned that there was a prejudice against the carrying
of the jack-knife. The laniard had to go round the neck,
which was said to make the wearer just like mother's
little sailor boy; and the knife had to tuck into the one
permitted outer breast pocket, in which a man had to

carry his handkerchief, money, and all other neces-
saries. There was really no room for the jack-knife.
Besides, for what should we need the knife? It was a
poor specimen of a knife, with one blade and no other
appliance. At sea, a sailor needs a knife, and can never
dare be without one. But our knives were not sailors'
knives. They had to be opened and shut. What sailor
can open and shut a knife when at work aloft in blowy
weather? A sheath-knife, worn at the back, where it will
not catch in any gear, is the only knife for a sailor.

However, it was now time to go down. My guides
told me to watch what they did, and to hold to the hand-
holds they showed me. I saw them swing themselves
outside the topmast rigging; bend; grope, as it were,
with a feeling foot, for the out of sight futtocks; then,
they were out of sight, below the top rim, calling to me
to come along. I quaked a little, but it was easier than
I had thought; the ratlines were easy to find; they were
there, at regular intervals, and my clutch on the hand-
holds was as tight as I could make it. In a few seconds,
I was down the futtocks, and in the rigging with my
guides. "It's not so bad, is it?" they said. "You'll soon
learn to run up and down. But remember; never put
your hands on ratlines. Either someone will tread on
them, or they'll carry away with you. Hold always to
the shrouds; then you'll be safe. And another thing.
Before you start to run down rigging, look down to
make sure the line's clear, or you may run into someone coming up and knock yourselves overboard. If you

don't do that, you'll kick him in the mouth; and he won't like it; it hurts like hell."

I came down from aloft well pleased with myself. My guides walked the deck with me, and sometimes told their friends that the chum had been aloft, and had not gone through the lubber's hole. Presently, we were piped to tea; I had to defend the mess butter with my life, after the repeated anguish of lifting the table down.

From the port of the mess, I could see the grand Cunarder at her buoy, with her lighters alongside; and much I longed to be her captain, at the top of the profession, instead of a measly pipsqueak of a new chum at the very bottom.

Red Swab called me from my place. "Come here," he said. "You see the maintop mess, there; No. 7 mess; three messes from here? They've got a mess treat. Take my plate to the second captain there, and say 'he promised me his spare,' then bring it back to me."

It was an order, and though I didn't know what was meant, I knew that any order must be obeyed on the instant; so I took his plate, and set off towards No. 7 mess. A mess treat was something as yet unknown to me; later, it was well known. It proceeded from various sources. Private generosity, thanksgiving for benefits received, or custom, made certain persons treat their messes to a feast. Certain promotions or glories imposed a mess treat; and all men, before leaving the ship, treated their messes. Old Conways, re-visiting the ship, always treated their old messes. The feasts were simple; ham and eggs, kippers, strawberries, sardines, sausages, tongues, and Eccles cakes, were the usual things provided. The mess captains arranged usually to hold the feast on some day when the ship's allowance, though always very liberal, was to boyish appetite somewhat lacking in charm. The buying of the dainties was left to a trusty hand, who was always given the half-hour ashore necessary for the purchase. The cooking of the food, if the thing had to be cooked, was arranged with one of the cooks; they would always do it, for value received, if not from good fellowship. Usually, they were jolly good fellows, and our friends.

The England of the early nineties was a land of cheapness; a mess treat, though seldom costly, was always very abundant, so that the mess found itself with twice as much as it could eat, and growing boys are not light eaters. It was the happy custom to let the abundance spill over. Members of a mess with a treat always "promised their spare", as it was called, to their friends, that is, they went halves with their chums, who called at the mess for it, and then sometimes dispensed of *their* spare to other friends, so that a mess treat was a time of good cheer to perhaps thirty, as a feast should be.

I went forth to No. 7 mess. A happy odour of kippers was diffused from the mess; and boys bearing gifts of kippers were hurrying back to their messes, with that glad stare with which a boy admires what he will soon enjoy. I was at the point of reaching the mess, when a man turning abruptly from the mess with a plate of given kippers ran into me. It was entirely his fault; the kippers were not spilt and no harm had been done. Still, he was a second-class P.O. and I was a new chum; that was much; and he was, unfortunately, the man into whom I had already butted twice that day; that was much more. He remembered the fact, as well as I did; and my eyes and other organs were cursed. "Run into me again," he called, "and I'll tear your, etc., etc." Although he bore a dish of happy kippers, he passed on snarling at me, and I, much abashed, for the condemnation was public, and publicly approved, quite forgot to ask leave to enter the mess. I entered it without permission.

"See here, chum," the captain of the mess said, "dirty new chums don't come into a maintop mess without asking leave. You go back, and tell your . . . Red Swab to teach his filthy focsle manners."

But here, the second captain interfered. "The kid only came aboard last night," he said.

"I don't care a damn," his chief said.

"No, but," the voice of reason pleaded, "let the chum off this time. See chum. You must never enter a mess without asking leave. Here's my spare for Red Swab; and some for you. I see you aren't a bad kid, only green. Gad, chum, you must drop your innocence aboard this —— hooker."

Well, this was true friendliness; and my heart warmed to this fine fellow who offered both kindness and a kipper, as it were, in one breath. In my emotion, I asked if I might leave the mess; and the big maintop-men laughed and told me to get to hell out of it.

After tea, one of my mess said: "We scrub decks to-morrow. You'd better keep off the orlop deck all you can this evening. The foretopmen fill their wash deck tubs, then; and they'll baptise you, if they catch you."

I asked what baptism meant, for indeed, most of what I had seen or heard of foretopmen, so far, seemed heathen.

"Well," my messmate said, "they put some chaps in head first, right down to the waist."

"So do the main," another said. "You'd better keep off this deck, too; for the main use barrels, not half-barrels; and they'll shove you in as far as you'll go."

This was not a cheering prospect; I had not thought that I could be baptised and then shoved in as far as I could go in one evening, between tea and bed. But someone spread a ray of hope. "They don't always baptise," he said. "Some evenings they don't do anybody." "Just after lecture is the worst time," they agreed.

There was to be a lecture, with a magic-lantern, that evening, as always, on Friday. I was advised to sit as far forward as I could get, near to the Captain, for then I might be let alone more.

I noticed that most of the focsles hung about the lower deck after tea that evening; baptism was in the air it seemed. There was nothing to do on the lower deck after we had swept, hoisted the cutter and coiled all ropes. It was now growing dark. The only solace was to stare at the Notice Boards under the big battle-lanterns. The ship's Watch and Station Bills were there; I read through these. Beside them, were large sheets of printed questions and answers in seamanship. I read these, not growing any wiser; for I did not yet know the language. One of the questions was: "What is a jumpsurgee strop?" It was a famous question on board, for the answer was not given; and though old Fleck explained the matter to us once, we forgot it, and perhaps he was the last man who knew. I read all the questions; many of them seemed to be about ear-rings, the inner and outer turns to be taken with ear-rings; the whole duty of a seaman seemed to be bound up in passing ear-rings with three inner and two outer; two outer and one inner; or three outer and as many inner as he could get. Suddenly, I heard my name called. I answered, though I felt sure, that this was my summons to the font. A maintopman, who had spoken to me once before, appeared. He asked me whether I could help him in a little matter. He was in the cutter, he said, and had still a run to make. Would I lend him my sea boots, just for the run, since his own were being repaired, and the top of the slip would certainly be under water. I could not possibly need the boots myself until the morning, and they would be back in my chest within five minutes of the cutter's return. He seemed a most dependable, friendly soul, and as I had seen that afternoon, during drill, a dashing smart seaman aloft. I was too green a hand to know that we had hoisted the cutter for the night, and that the man was lying. I took him down to my chest, pulled out my sea boots, and lent them to him. I noticed, as I did so, that their side-straps were of coarse stuff. My friend said he would put them back in my chest directly the cutter returned.

It being known that I had a little tuck still, various men applied for some. Giving is a main delight in life, but the process is happier when left to the giver. I was thinking on these lines, when a man suddenly fell upon my beggars and told them they ought to be ashamed to rob a kid in that way. He was a man of much probity and very great physical strength, not clever, but a fine seaman. When he had scattered the beggars, he asked me to mooch with him. "A new chum needs some advice," he said. This he proceeded to give as we walked the orlop, where I saw some fonts already prepared for at least a sprinkling. He told me that a lot of new chums complained of their first terms, but that they really did not know when they were well off. "It's when you're youngest hand in a top that you'll want to squeal," he said.

Soon, we were called to the main deck, to the lecture. At that time, and for some terms longer, lectures were always given on the main deck. I was very soon shown that a place near the Captain's chair was not for me. I took a modest place and prepared to enjoy the hour. So did some maintopmen just behind me. They told me that if I made the least sound during the lecture I might just as well jump overboard, for the Skipper would never forgive any interruption during a lecture. I thanked them for telling me, and said that I should keep very quiet. They said: "I'd better"; and as the lecture began, so did my kind friends. One, with a skilled and strong finger fillipped my right ear; the other, my left; and the ears had hardly recovered from the shock, when it was repeated and repeated, being sometimes varied with neat little upward tweaks of my hair. It was excruciating, but it had to be borne. If I made the least noise, there was the Skipper, ready to devour me; and if he failed, there were these maintopmen. Either way, I knew that I might just as well jump overboard. Neither of my tormentors paid any attention to the lecture, but during applause, they cheered, and gave my unhappy ears a tug or two. "Never mind the naughty maintopmen," they said, during some irruption of applause, "we'll put you in the barrel afterwards, and that'll cool your ears down nicely." I had not thought that they could be so heartless as to wreck my evening and then put me into a barrel; but the prospect seemed to delight them both.

It was a horrible evening, but, like other horrible times, it ended. The Captain made one of his admirable speeches of thanks, while I quaked with the thought: "Now I shall be put in the barrel, as far as I can go."

To my astonishment and relief, my topmen made no effort to keep me for a ducking; I was allowed to go. Men told me that it was a jolly fine lecture. During the

brief remainder of the day, I waited for raiders seeking
candidates for baptism. I could hear, and sometimes
saw them at "their priest-like task" of filling up tubs
for the morrow; somehow, they were not baptising that
night. (I never was baptised, in either kind of tub.) I
swept my deck; and then the man who had borrowed
my sea boots found me and took me to mooch. He said
that he had put back my boots in my chest. He seemed
most uneasy about something. He kept repeating that
he had done "a dirty thing, this night; a dirty, dirty
thing". When I said that I was sure he hadn't, he said,
he had, and that he was surely a dirty hound.

The pipe went, for divisions for hammocks; the
nightmare of the night before was to begin. Washing
and hammock times were always the worst for new
chums; I already dreaded them. The scene was interesting. Those long lines of silent seamen, with their
hands out; and the lantern light held an instant upon
each man's face were images which I have never forgotten; and now illustrate for me some centuries of sea
custom. From this quiet I hurried to the dim, smelly
cave of the hold, where chaos came roaring and eyes
got well——.

Everybody found me in the way, everybody knocked
me aside, and all —— my eyes and my insides; a big
man, grabbing his hammock and running with it,
would scatter me into somebody's way; the somebody
would smite or kick and say these chums need —— well

skinning. Still, somehow, I found my bag of misery; it seemed even clumsier and heavier than I remembered, but I got it, and shouldered it, and went up the ladder with it, and at every other step, as it seemed, I did something wrong, or got in someone's way, and was asked who in hell I thought I was and where in hell I was coming? By the time I reached the orlop deck, I did not know the answer to either question, but judged that the answer to both began "in hell". When I reached the orlop deck, I looked out for that grim nook by the furnace where the terrible second-class P.O. slung, the one who had now —— me thrice. If I ran into him a fourth time . . . ? He was there, busy with his hammock and did not see me, but two other devils did; they charged out from their fastness from behind me, and with a vigorous push sent me flying into the main hatch. I fell against this, and the hatch supported me so that I didn't come down, but by the time I was moving again, my two attackers were gone; I know not who they were. After this, I reached my place, got my crank down and proceeded to sling my hammock.

While I was busy spreading my bedding, a sympathetic friend stood at my crank, saying how wise I was to give up my impossible sheets and saying, too, that I had done very well for a new chum, only one day aboard, and that I should soon get into the way of things. He was a mizentopman, and a senior. I was touched at his kindness and understanding. Suddenly, he left me and went forward to his top, and almost at the same instant my hammock collapsed on to the deck. While he had talked to me, he had subtly undone my hitch, and had passed a slippery hitch in its stead. I reslung the hammock, marvelling that man could be so deceitful, and this to his brother man, his shipmate.

After main deck Prayers, Red Swab very kindly said that he hoped I should be able to turn in smartly now. I hoped so too, and meant to try. Alas, when I came to my hammock, it had been emptied right out upon the deck, and then twisted up upon itself, like several other hammocks, by hands unknown, who had probably not been at Prayers, or had certainly not profited by them. I had to make my hammock when I ought to have been undressing; and again Red Swab was vexed, and made me turn in half-undressed, so that he could report me "in." After Rounds, Red Swab let me turn out and undress properly.

At last, I was snug abed; my first day aboard was over. It had been the longest and the strangest day I had ever known, with much in it intensely interesting; much, delightful, but nearly all of it bewildering, incomprehensible. Certainly, the best of the men were finer fellows than any I had met or dreamed of. The school work, as far as I could judge from my taste of it, seemed exactly suited to my powers, which tended, perhaps, somewhat, towards indolence. But it was an odd world; I was off my feet; and felt lost.

However, the great thing was, that a day of it was over; H.B. came to his hammock beside me. As he swiftly undressed, he asked me how I had got on during the day. I said: "All right, thanks."

"A bit odd at first," he said, "but you'll soon get the hang of it. Have you been aloft yet?"

"Yes."

"How far did you get?"

"The cross-trees."

"Come, that's first rate for a first attempt. But you won't want to go aloft after this term. You'll have too much drill aloft for that."

"Shall I ever have to go up to the very top of the mast?"

"The truck? No, you won't *have* to go; but everybody does go, at some time."

"To stand on it?"

"Stand on it? No fear, just to touch it and say you've touched it, or to rest your chin on it and say you've looked over it."

"Would it be possible to stand on it?"

"But, chum, it's only a wooden disc about nine inches across, with nothing to hold on to, but the sky."

"I've read of a boy standing on one in some frigate."

"How did he get down?"

"He jumped."

"Was he killed?"

"No. He went overboard."

"I suppose he jumped sideways then," H.B. said, reckoning the chances. "If he jumped forward, he would have been killed. I suppose the ship was at anchor?"

"Yes."

"I suppose most people could get on to a truck," H.B. said, "if they cared to run the risk; it's the getting down that would be the trouble. Falling sideways you would have some small chance; the rigging might tip you over the side; and the same if you fell backwards, perhaps."

"Here, you would go into the net, I suppose?" I said.

"Yes, but from that height you would fall with such force that you might go through the net; it would break the fall, of course. What made your boy stand on the truck?"

"He did it for fun."

"Don't you do it for fun. But I'll find out about it tomorrow. If it has been done, there are men aboard here who will know about it. I'll ask. But it could only be done to show your hand and head. Now and then, about once a year, perhaps, some ambitious soul here goes up to the main truck, lies flat upon it, takes off his coat and flings it down. There's always some sort of wind stirring, up there, and the coat goes overboard; that's all you get by it."

"Is it against the rules?"

"Not that I know of. It's done; but hardly ever. An officer would have to decide, whether the man was being smart or silly; it would all lie in that of course. But, come on, now! this is enough of the truck. Heave round on some ghost yarn; that is much better fun than standing on a truck."

I "hove round" on the ghost yarn; I had many still to spin.

Well, even of ghost yarns, even H.B. had enough at last. He had wrung my hand, as before, tucked himself up and fallen asleep, it seemed, in five seconds; and there I was again, with the strangeness of everything, the light, the gurgling tide, and the cable grinding. Then these things merged, and I was asleep, until, with a rattle and bang, my hammock struck the deck; I had been "let down" again.

I had been told to dress next morning with jumper and sea boots. When all hands were called I ran to fetch my sea boots from my chest; and lo, when I pulled them out, they were not mine. Mine had had brightness, newness, and coarse stuff handles; these in my chest were old, dull, torn across one toe, and fitted with rubber-handles. It was clear that my friend had stolen my boots and left his ruins instead. This was a bitter blow.

"Never mind about that, now," Dick said. "Get your hammock down; get washed; and see the chap about it before breakfast."

I did mind about it, though, as I tried to lash my hammock. Now I knew what the dirty thing was that had smitten his conscience the night before. With a heavy heart I tried to get my bedding rolled tightly, and to pass my seven turns. The result was pretty bad, but I got it done, unhooked the bundle, tucked the

clues and with difficulty got the thing hoisted. I went
off with it, towards the hold and as I tottered, came
across the path of men of the port watch, now returning
from the lavatory. The chance of knocking a new chum
over, as he tottered with a hammock was much too good
to miss. They charged me over, and cursed me for getting in their way; they flicked me with their wet towels;
they —— my cheek for coming into the top without
leave. These —— new chums, they said were getting
so —— uppish, they thought they ran the ship.

But all these griefs, keenly felt at the moment, were
nothing to the grief in the hold, when the second captain asked me what the —— I thought my package was;
was I carrying guts to the bears, or what? I said, it was
my hammock. "Don't tell me," he said, "that's not a
hammock. That doesn't go into one of my racks. Take
it up and lash it properly, if it's a hammock; then, perhaps, I'll see about it. Out you go, now. Don't stand
blocking the gangway there. Up and lash it."

At this moment, a foretopman with a face both
thoughtful and kind took pity on me. He sang out to
the second captain: "Let me give the kid a hand here."
He very kindly slung my bundle to the racks, and with
a few deft punches and twitches had the thing properly
lashed in a minute. "You see?" he said, "it's all done by
kindness. That's all it is. You'll be able to do that tomorrow, won't you?" I thanked him from my heart, but
was not at all sure about being able to do it on the morrow, or, indeed, ever. When it was lashed, I was allowed

to stow it, and having stowed it, became conscious that I must rush to the lavatory, for the pipe "Starboard watch to the lavatory," had long since sounded. I was wearing the torn sea boots of the maintopman; and these caught the eyes of the critics. "Look at that chum's sea boots," they said, "what's Red Swab thinking of, to let his chums wear boots like that?"

"—— little hound," one said, "you swiped those boots from Paddy Doyle."

Washing was as weary a time as it had been the day before. I had to wait till nearly everyone had gone, and then had my eyes —— by the captains of the lavatories, "for keeping everybody waiting."

As I ran down to my chest afterwards, I met my friend the maintopman, wearing my sea boots. I said I was so glad to meet him, for there was some mistake about my sea boots; he hadn't returned my pair, but another pair. I was afraid that he would deny that there had been a mistake; but, no; he said, "Indade there had"; and with much good nature, and no beastly false shame kicked off my boots, so that I might have them and took his old torn pair. Whatever pangs the morning had brought, this restoration of the boots made many amends. I had hoped to go aloft before breakfast; somebody told me not to do this in sea boots, as the ratlines cut the rubber so.

Scrubbing decks, or cleaning ship, was the work of Saturday morning; we had no school whatever. As soon as the launch had been coaled, and the deck swept we began with a pumping of water till the deck was awash. We were then put to heavy, long-handled scrubbers, more weight than bristle, and scrubbed the entire deck in line. After us, came other lines of men with hard brooms and buckets, "brooming down" into the scuppers. After these, came the swabbers. It was all wet and jolly, but the best of the fun came later, when we got hot water from the galley, and soft soap from Dick and started on the paint-work.

I was thrilled to enter the galley. I knew that the range had been in the *Great Eastern* and must often have echoed to the knocks of the riveter's ghost. I had been told, too, that the cooks had been chefs in P. & O. liners. The cook who gave me the hot water had certainly been in the East. When excited, he used Hindustani words of forceful kinds, which some men added to their already good collections of such things. He was exceedingly kind to new chums always and never minded our coming for hot water.

Dick set me to wash the bulkheads and jalousies of the bathrooms and storerooms, and allotted as companion the focsleman I most disliked. This man expected me to do all the work, as I was "youngest hand"; but I was beginning to learn that the youngest hand, even he, had rights. As we cleaned, I asked this man when we should use these baths? He said: "Whenever you ask leave and care to pump the water. If you've been coaling, you'll have to clean the paint-work before they'll let you out."

Here, Dick looked in, to say that we weren't there for conversation, but to clean paint. "Come on out, you," he said. "I'll put you where you can't talk quite so much."

He set me to clean parts of the ship's side, and the great yellow waterways; it was then that I began to know that the ship's air of shiny, speckless cleanness was due to hard work and pride in her crew. I began to take pleasure in helping to smarten her up.

Certain splashings of soapy water had to be swilled away; then Dick told me to nip forward and fetch the squeegees. I did not know what he meant; he repeated: "In the manger; the squeegees," as though any fool must know squeegees. I knew the manger, of course; so, looking into it, I saw some odd things still in the racks, and as there was nothing else there, I judged that these were they; as they were.

I was put to a squeegee. The delight of using a squeegee has seldom been properly sung by poets. The supposed reference in . . .

Alas, my joy in the poetry of squeegees was cut short. Dick remembered that the swabs had not been wrung out, and put the youngest hand to that hated job at the foot of the gangway. This time I had to wring them.

After this, all hands turned to upon the staunchions and the brass, while an Instructor, helped by two criminals on the black list, touched up the ranged cables with some shiny black stuff, which dried at once and left a heavy aromatic smell.

When we had finished our brightwork, the deck was almost dry from the sun and the blowing wind; it looked most beautiful. I looked at it with the feeling that it owed some of its appearance to me; I was proud of it. "Deck," as Napoleon might have put it, "the Emperor is content with you." But (as Napoleon might have added) "Much remains to be done." All the glass of the ports needed the dry dusters, and then all the falls, of three cutters and the dinghy; and all the boom inhauls and outhauls had to be neatly coiled down, clear for running, on the now dry deck.

After this, I was sent below, to change into uniform, tidy up, and get my week's washing ready.

When I got below, most of the ship's company was there already, for no deck took so long as ours. The men were more or less naked, exceedingly merry, and for once, leisurely. They had brought white, canvas kit-bags from their chests and into these they packed their soiled linen. On printed clothes lists they entered whatever they were sending, and put the list on the top of the gear. They then shook down the clothing to the foot of the bag, lashed the laniard round the neck, and at once used the bag as a club on any convenient head; mine was there just for that.

Then, too, in the maintop, a woad parade was being judged. Some of our blue clothing, the "Crimea" shirts, especially, yielded much blue dye when wet. Some men in warm weather wore these things on Saturdays, so that they might be woaded over when they came down to change. Amid a good deal of ribaldry, they held a woad parade, dancing naked before the judges; it was not familiar to me then, these blue marine deities disporting.

Presently, our washing-bags were stowed into big, canvas-covered baskets, and dragged aboard the launch for the shore. That ended the Saturday morning routine. We had still twenty minutes before dinner.

I had proposed to my friend that we should go aloft; we were about to go, when we were confronted and stopped by three big maintopmen, all of them rated, and all of the port watch. I had seen the three together more than once; they were always together; and I had not liked their looks. The biggest, who was a giant, was a big rumbustious rowdy fellow, rather like a playful bull; the next biggest was a much cleverer man; he had brains; he looked like the leader of a criminal gang in a successful film; the third had the sort of face which made the new chum's blood run cold. "Here are these three," said my friend, "now we're done." The three bore down upon us and checked our way. "Chums, by ——," the third man said. "What are your names, chums?"

We told our names, but that was only the beginning; we were put through an inquisition, and then through a psycho-analysis; one or two burly idlers, friends of the board, hove to alongside, to listen with some mild amusement.

Presently, they seemed to weary of our answers. The

third man ended the questioning by resuming his companion's arms. "So now I know all about it," he said, "by ——, I learn something new every day." With this the three moved off round the deck, with the indescribable lazy, slouching swagger of three old hands.

I had been told that I could go ashore that afternoon if I wished, to the football field, with the other juniors. I thought that this might be fun. At the end of dinner, when the tables had been hooked up, the Officer of the Day gave the orders. "The port main will man the cutter. The dinghies will man their boat. Seniors to the Baths. Juniors to the Field. Clear up decks. Dismiss."

There was the usual scurry, to sweep the decks; then at the pipe of Liberty Men Fall In on the lower deck; we stood in divisions while the Officer of the Day inspected us to see if we were smart enough to be allowed ashore. The seniors, who were going to Liverpool to the Baths, went ashore first, so that they might catch the steamer: we juniors followed. We crowded into the launch; it was still a new delight to make a run in a steam launch, either sitting on deck or jammed into her cabin. We came ashore at Rock Ferry Slip, up which I went for the first time. All the men in my launch load were new chums. They told me that the slip shop, which served as the ship's tuck shop, was at the head of the slip, but that I need not think that I should be able to buy anything there; "It'll be all full of seniors." One said to me, that we had better run past the shop before we were caught, because lots of seniors lay in wait for new chums for pony racing. I asked what this meant. "You'll jolly soon learn," they said. "They catch you and make you carry them pickaback along the Promenade, and race you against someone." This was confirmed by others.

The slip was then, as it perhaps still is, a strong sloping pier, ending in pretty deep water. It was well named. It was exceedingly slippery when the tide ebbed. It was of a reddish and greyish stone, often greenish with sea slime, and worn into pools and hollows. It had let into it various big iron mooring-hooks and rings, all rusty and slimy. Now and then a schooner or other small craft lay alongside, discharging cargo. Our cutters called there daily, often many times in the day, for mails, passengers, provisions, and for the going and coming of the ship's staff, and the Skipper's family. At the head of the slip, near the iron gates, where passengers had once bought tickets for the ferries, my messmates showed me a sort of hinged door. They told me that when it was swung back, it showed a conspicuous mark easily visible by the officer of the watch on board. It meant that someone wanted a boat, but that woe betide any new chum or junior who went proclaiming that he wanted a boat. From this point, to my right, they showed me the slip shop, a tiny place, plainly not for the likes of us. It was full to overflowing with the noisy and the godless. Terrible old hands were within, rousing the afternoon with cat-calls, chaff and scuffle. "Come on, now," said my messmates, "now's our chance; run now, and sharp round to the left along the Esplanade." We did not want to be ponies carrying heavy seniors for six hundred yards, even on the flat; we ran for it. We heard some of the pirates shouting at us from the door, but we paid no attention to them; we ran and ran. I asked, "Where is the field?" My mates said: "Run. Run." Looking back, a few moments later, I saw the elements of a pony race in progress; and knew that some witless ones had either not run or had not run fast enough.

It had puzzled me that no one in the ship, so far, had shown the least interest in any game. No man had been pointed out to me as a cricketer or football player. No man of those with whom I ran had any interest in the game to which, as I supposed, we were running. In fact, our company was strangely dwindled, a good many men having taken less open ways than the Esplanade. In theory half the ship's company should have been going to the field; some eighty or ninety men; what had happened to them?

We hurried along the Esplanade, with the sea wall and the beach on one hand, and a land wall and weather-bitten trees on the other. As always, the River looked superb. My friends told me something of the three other training ships lying in the line with us; a line-of-battle-ship, slightly smaller than ourselves, a fine frigate, and then another line-of-battle-ship. The ships of the line were reformatories so-called; we sometimes wondered how many they reformed.

I remember well, that at one point, the sea wall had been washed away. My friends said that that was a terrible place in pony racing; they called it Beecher's Brook.

However, in a few minutes, we were round the bend, and out of sight of the river, and in a minute more were at the field.

I had expected a levelled, rolled field, marked out into perhaps three different football fields, each with touch lines and goal posts. I had not doubted, that the ship's eleven would be there, playing some local school, or some eleven of Liverpool; there would be a pavilion, with dressing-rooms; and those of us not able to take part in any game, for want of room on the field, would line the touch lines, and cheer the ship's eleven.

I was shocked, when we reached the reality; it was not what I had expected in any way. Liverpool then was often a very smoky city; a certain blackness or dinginess of smoke descended from her upon the surrounding country. New Ferry was visibly blackened thus; the trees and the grass were dirty. The field, to which we had come, was a somewhat narrow, long, sloping stretch of blackened grass: it had the double slope, a long droop towards the river, and a sideways tilt towards what had been a brook. It had no part of it levelled; it had never been rolled; it was unprepared in any way for any game whatever; it had no goal posts, no pavilion; it was a rough wild field, with grim grass, and stunted, blackened thorn bushes. When we ar-

rived, I wondered why we had come. What game were
we to play? We had no appliances, no ball, even. One
of the men said that one of the Instructors would presently bring us a ball, and that if we rolled up our tunics
they would do for goal posts. We were now less than
a dozen men, all told, all new chums.

I knew that some unfortunates had been caught as
ponies. What could have become of all the other juniors, I asked. A pitying messmate said that some of
them had contrived to go on to the Baths, or at least
to the Landing Stage, in the hope of not being spotted,
and that others had slipped away into Rock Ferry somewhere, to have a walk and smoke, before working back
to the slip shop in time for the cutter. I was such a new
chum that these things seemed to me to be crimes. I
determined to wait for the ball and to play, if a game
were possible. While I waited, some of the dozen
slipped away, leaving only seven for football. An Instructor presently reached us with a ball. He said that
when we had finished playing we could leave the ball
at a certain house, and that we were to be at the slip for
the cutter at a certain time. He left us, then, to play.
But two of my messmates, my seniors, said that they
were not going to play football in their best go-ashore
uniforms, nor to make their boots filthy, so that it
would take them half an hour to clean up, when they
got aboard. They said that they were going for a walk;
the elder of the two, the moralist, the man who always
asked me what I was gaping at, now asked me if I would

walk with them? This seemed friendly as well as sensible. The other four who didn't seem to mind getting their uniforms filthy began to kick the ball to and fro. When kicked, it trended down one or other of the slopes. We left them to this joy, and walked inland, all determined never to visit the field again. We never did, nor, during my time aboard, was it ever made more attractive.

We walked on, talking of our new strange life, and of the various dangerous characters on board who ought to be avoided when possible. We walked far, and talked long, when we suddenly noticed that time had passed, and that we were far from the slip and the cutter. We were aghast. We should miss the cutter; we should be reported; all three of us, new chums, would have black marks upon our records; as my enemy said, "we shall lose our good names". We did not know how criminal the officers would think us; we expected not less than a week of black list each. We had heard of black list, but did not know what it meant. Pretty grim, "A week of black list," after less than two days aboard; it sounded like ruin.

We did not know Rock Ferry, but could see the general lie of the River, and started to run towards that. We were all good runners, and fear spurred us. Some kind passer, to whom we appealed, showed us that we were on the long straight road leading to the slip. I kept my breath for running; my enemy kept groaning that we should lose our good names; the third kept saying that it would be a terrible thing to tell his mother. We ran our best, and lo, as we drew near, we saw the boat's oars toss and collapse at the slip end, as the boat came in and made fast. "There's the cutter, I do believe," my enemy said, "we're saved."

We were now passing the slip shop. An idler at the door of it asked us what was all the rally about; and called to those within to come and look at the filthy chums. Somewhat shamed by this, we lapsed into a walk. We dared not try to enter the shop; we walked down the slip and there found the dinghy in charge of the third or dangerous maintopman who had waylaid me that morning. We asked if we might go off in his boat. He said: "Yes, if you care to wait; stow yourselves forward, somewhere out of smell." When we were stowed, we kept silence, for it was not for us to talk unless spoken to.

The P.O. looked as though he was not and never had been young. He had a pale, hard face, a mouth which looked as if it had worn loose from constant spitting of tobacco juice, and hard, grey, observant eyes, with the sea look in them, of watching the sky for the sign of a shift of wind. He seemed to me to have been at sea for years. Lolling in the stern-sheets, chewing tobacco, spitting with much skill over the gunwale, and batting his shanks with the tiller, he eyed the River and the shipping, with occasional comment, usually professional, and always profane. I thought him a dreadful fellow, and a terrible influence. Presently, we were joined by a long and spry maintopman, who held a second-class rate of some sort; I had seen him and heard him; now, I was to know him a little. He hailed the dinghy with easy cheer, and curled himself up in the stern-sheets. "What have you got forward, there?" he asked.

"Oh, some —— chums or other."

"I thought from their looks they were pigs."

"Yes, you might; and from their smell. Dammee, dammee; when's the mail master going to bring his parcels down?"

"You won't see him for half an hour yet."

There were some more oaths, and the time slowly passed. We watched the River in its extraordinary beauty. I looked at the wreck just upstream, where such frightful fates had fallen. The newcomer began to sing an indecent song, to which we all lent attentive ears. The pirate in charge of us smiled approval.

"So that was that?" he said. "Sing us another."

He sang another, equally new to me. For the next few months, I heard snatches of it daily; its novelty was its chief merit. Feeling that it had not been a great success, he began upon a third, a much older and much less proper song, with a rousing good tune and chorus, in which (although we were only new chums) he expected us to join. It delighted us all. We trembled a little, for its wickedness, and yet, to know the wickedness, and to dare it, was not this being at sea?

After the songs, came talk about the inner life of the

ship, concerning men not yet known to me, even by name. After a while, the four who had stayed at the field came down, and asked if they might go off in the dinghy. The pirate in command looked at their muddy boots, and said, with much disgust. "No; you can wait for the launch. We had to clean this hooker this morning. You're not going to bring those boots aboard here; don't think it."

The mail master came down, eating a delicacy which was much in favour among the ship's company. It was called Italian Cream; it was, perhaps, made by the keepers of the slip shop, for I never saw it elsewhere. It was exceedingly good either in its pink or its white form, and for a food so exquisite it was very cheap. The mail master had his leather bag of parcels slung over his shoulder, and his foot of Italian Cream slowly diminishing by bites in his hand. "Buck up," our pirate said.

"Why, what's the rally?" the mail master answered. "Come on and have some cream."

There was no beastly class pride about the mail master; he shared his cream like a white man; he gave us new chums a share. He seemed to radiate happy repletion, though he said, "I expect I shall be sick tonight." Our pirate said "Shove off, there. Let go forrard; jump in aft. Back a stroke; you."

The bowman, shoving her off, told me to sit small, and not to get in his way. It was a new delight to be in a ship's boat, rowed by shipmates; and I must say that I enjoyed the journey. I was terrified none the less by the pirate who steered. "Come; toss her up; toss her up," he cried; then came an oath or two; and a sideway squirt of tobacco juice; and all this, with a haggard look of having been at sea in foul weather for the last seventeen years, yet still keeping undaunted, untamed, looking to windward and able to damn the crew. How could anyone be so tough, I wondered, unless pickled in salt water from birth? Towards the end of the journey, he dropped his used quid overboard, and took a tauter line with his rowers. "Come, toss her up. Toss her up, you filthy cripples," he called. "Rally her alongside; not like this. Toss her up." At this, the crew put their weights on, and did toss her up, so as to come alongside in style. We went aboard, and reported our arrival; we were half an hour earlier than we need have been, but, then, our good names had been saved.

In all my time on board, I did not again visit the field. I was told that in the summer term another field was provided for cricket; I never saw it, nor did I ever see any match played by the ship's cricket and football elevens. It was borne in upon me from the first that these things were done by boys, and that we were now men, seafaring men. Of course, living in the ship as we did, the getting ashore to any field, took time, and the use of boats and their crews. Then, games, especially in the winter, may make boys very muddy, and to expect boys to be smart in uniform, boots, collars and caps, on leaving the ship, and to be still smart when returning aboard, after rolling in the mud, is expecting a good deal. No man who had cleaned out a cutter in the forenoon wanted muddy boots all over her a few hours later. No man, who had spent ten minutes smartening for going ashore, wished to spend half an hour later, cleaning up.

My sight of the field was the cause of much perplexity to me. I had come to a community with ways utterly unlike anything I had known or imagined, where men liked chewing tobacco and loathed new chums, where no one cared twopence if cricket or football dropped to the bottomless pit, but cared a great deal for neatness, cleanliness and smartness; cared nothing at all, seemingly, for books, and were not pressed to learn anything from books, but cared enormously for food, and for any art which might bring food; where prowess at books or games did not seem to matter, but where arbitrary divisions, watches, seniorities, tops and messes, were life itself.

One good result of my going ashore had been that I had seen the mail master, who was, as I had learned, first over the Library. He had shared his Italian Cream with me, almost as though I had belonged to the same planet; he had seemed a very decent fellow. So summoning up my courage, I went to him, after tea, and asked if I might ever go into the Library. He said: "Of course. You've only just come aboard, haven't you? The subscription, for newspapers, is eighteenpence a term.

I'll collect that from you during the term. Have you
been in the Library?"

"No, not yet."

"Well, come in, and see it." He led me aft along the
port side of the lower deck, to what was then the
Library, a bulkheaded space shutting off the stern and I
think three other after gun ports, and extending amidships, where a bulkhead shut it from the Sick Bay. My
guide said, "When you reach the door here, you must
ask leave. You must say, 'May I come in the Library,
please?' One of the P.O.'s over the Library is always
here, and he'll give you leave. And you won't be
allowed to play the fool in here, for the Sick Bay is just
the other side of that bulkhead, and Joey, the Chaplain,
on the other side of that one. You can take out one book
at a time, if you get the P.O. to enter it and show that
you've returned the last."

As he was first over the Library, he could enter without leave. He called to the P.O. whose watch it was
there. "Here's a new chum for you," and then left me.

I was often in the Library during my time on board.
For about a month, long afterwards, at a busy season, I
was even fifth or supernumerary P.O. over it. I entered
it with hope and expectation, as well as with interest. I
had never been in that part of the ship, and every part,
so far, had been exciting.

The place was spotlessly clean; all the white paint
was glossy and shiny. A horsehair lounge or divan ran
along the ship's side under the ports. From the stern

port, one had a view of the rudder, with the floating man-catcher below it, which during my time on board, saved a man from drowning. In the midst of the room was a table, with forms and chairs for the readers, and a fair selection of daily and weekly papers. On the forward bulkhead were the shelves of the library, to which I turned with eagerness.

It was a very odd collection of books, some of them religious, some geographical, a good many technical, and perhaps fifty works of feeble fiction, gathered none knew how, perhaps left by Old Conways. Among the lower shelves, were strange, ruinous bound folios of illustrated magazines of the time of the Crimean War. In the course of time, I got to know the collection pretty well, for the Library, in case of any epidemic, became a part of the Sick Bay, and during two epidemics I lived there for a fortnight. When I was fifth over it, my time was mostly passed in trying to keep the place spotless, or in going out as mail master. On the midship bulkhead, I noticed particularly a pencil drawing of a fully rigged ship in a howling gale and some of the disorder of disaster. A note told what ship she was, the date of the storm, and the fact that "an ex-Conway boy had gone aloft, axe in hand, and saved both ship and crew," I suppose, by cutting something adrift.

The P.O. told me that I probably shouldn't want to take out any book to read, since I could just as well read there as elsewhere, but that I could if I liked. The main treasure of the Library, and plainly the work most read, were the bound volumes of a professional magazine. I looked at one of the volumes, hoping for some crumb of the bread of life. I found more evidence of the depth and completeness of my ignorance. There were articles on compensating magnets, on the merits of different anti-fouling mixtures, on some new invention of Lord Kelvin's, or some old dodge of Master Mariner's or Middle Watch's. I knew not what was meant. I did not know the language; it was all foreign to me. I looked at two of the books, and remember that in one of them there was an account of tacking ship with the mainsail not hauled up; and, in the other, many incomprehensible hints about clapping burtons here or there, and setting them well taut, before doing this or that.

Plainly, I could get nothing from books like these, and nothing from the printed questions on the notice board, till I had mastered the grammar and learned the speech.

There were chessmen and draughts for those who wished. I remember being bitterly disappointed with the Library because I could see no book to help my ignorance. Not knowing the laws of this strange world, and fearing to make a mistake, I asked if I might leave it? At this, there was a general laugh, which taught me not to ask another time.

I went out, and wandered where I was not wanted, and so, at last, came to the main deck, where I found the real life of the ship.

I was not homesick; I was not unhappy, only completely lost in a new world.

On the main deck, many happy men had pulled out desks and forms under the heavy, swinging copper lamps; some were reading or writing; some, netting hammocks in macramé string; others, matting; some, carving; about three of the silent workers little groups of men stood intently watching what was being done. I timidly asked another new chum, who had all the superiority of fourteen days seniority what was the interest of the nearest group. He said: "It's . . . , doing a ship in a setting-in book." I asked if I might be allowed to look. He said: "Yes, if you don't get too close." I had learned enough of the ship's life not to do that, so I peered cautiously, and perceived a senior, whom I had noticed already elsewhere, drawing a ship in full sail on the page of an exercise book. He was using a crow-quill pen and a little china pan of Indian ink. I was not skilled enough to know whether the ship were like a ship; to me, she seemed instinct with truth and grace; she was lifting and flying. The artist seemed to see her in every detail and to draw her easily with the hand of power. All the dozen men watching him felt as I did, that we were watching a miracle; each one of us longed to be somehow in a position of seniority or friendship which might ask for, or purchase, such another work of art.

I went cautiously to see the work of the other artists; one of them was painting in water colour. He was a senior, who, seeing my evident adoration of his genius, supposed that I might be intelligent, and asked if I painted. I said: "No; I was afraid not."

"You ought to paint," he said, "every sailor ought to paint; or at any rate make records in neutral tint . . ."

"Please, will you tell me what that is?"

"It's very simple; a little blue, a little red, and a little brown, all mixed. Did you ever see a setting-in book?"

"No; never."

He held up the book in which he was painting, slantingly to the light, so that he could be sure that the page was dry; he then handed it to me. "This is a setting-in book," he said. "You set into it examples of how you work out your different sights. Generally, you don't begin one till you're a Quarter Boy, but if you're wise, you'll start one now."

I looked at the book with interest and admiration; and at once began to long for one of my own; for it was not only a record of knowledge painfully won and exquisitely written down, but an album, illustrated by the choicest artists in the ship, and made precious by the signatures and apothegms of eminent officers and shipmates. One such sentence caught my eye; it was signed by one whom I already knew to be the toughest character on board: "Love is sweeter than sugar."

In itself, the setting-in book was a handsome large quarto manuscript book, having unlined pages of choice paper, and strongly bound in some black leathery substance. It cost about seven shillings and sixpence. Into this, with great care, with much careful ruling, and the occasional use of coloured inks, the man "set-in" or wrote out examples of every calculation by which a ship's position could be determined. If the owners were keen seamen, and many men were, they did not stop at Navigation; they added Meteorology, Rule of the Road, and even interesting points of seamanship. When a book had been filled by a conscientious man, he had learned much. Of course, during his next few years at sea, he forgot much, but if he kept his book it was of the utmost use to him before going up to pass for second mate. More than once in after years, Old Conways asked me for the loan of my book, so that they might have a guide to the various problems. I believe that it is now many years since setting-in books were brought to an end, having served their turn. On the whole, in my time, they were among the best things in the ship; they made the gathering of knowledge a work of art, and brought art to the gracing of knowledge.

I was amazed at the friendliness of the artists. One of the netters invited me to try my hand at netting, and this, though he had made his delicate and brittle gear with his own hands. The chief carver was another miracle of a man. He had a pen-knife and some hard wood from which he was making a "luff-tackle". I did not know what that was, but could see the kind of thing, and marvelled at the patient power and delicate firmness which shaped shells, pins and sheaves, then stropped the completed blocks, rove off his falls, hooked on, and at last hoisted some little load from the deck. I was happy to be with men so sensible who knew the right uses of power.

On the upper deck, just above my head, some fifty men were mooching round in a rather quick time, singing the old and indelicate song which I had heard that afternoon. They marched to it, in linked groups of three or four, arm in arm, stamping with their feet and making all the noise they could. All through the rest of that term, that song was the song of the ship on every cold, fine night.

While I was enjoying this evening, admiring the works of genius, I heard my name shouted, and then repeated, in what was then the ship's way, with my initials. Wondering what I had done wrong, or what wrong was about to be done to me, I answered the hailer, whom I saw, to my horror, to be the Captain of the Hold, the black haired, grim-looking man, who had been so savage about my hammock. My heart sank; I was sure that I was now going to be taken into the hold, and shown, that if I wanted my hammock to be among its Christian fellows, it would have to go through the eye of the needle, that is, the gauging-hoop. I was surprised, when the grim man appeared all smiles. He was a very smart man in his appearance. He shone; his hair gleamed; he was wearing his best tunic, with new gold lace stripes, and held himself well. He said: "Chum; I expect you've heard about the League. There's no compulsion to join it, but most men do. It's a promise to avoid drinking and smoking, etc., and the Skipper's very keen on new chums joining, if they can. Would you like to come along now, and see the Skipper about it; he's in his office here? You'd much better join."

I had read that most men joined, and as I had no temptation whatever to the four delights I was asked to eschew, I said I would join. "That's right," he said, "that'll please the Skipper; come along." It had puzzled me since I had come aboard to find that the promise to avoid swearing was not kept with rigorous strictness by all the members of the League; this was the sea life coming out, I suppose. I followed the Captain of the Hold into a dark Armoury, in which rifles and cutlasses gleamed from their racks. At an open, lamp-lit cabin door, the C.H. tapped, and on being told to enter, drew me in. "I've brought him in sir," he said, "he would like to join."

The Skipper was seated at his desk. I have been told, but cannot vouch for it, that long afterwards he died at that very spot. He greeted me kindly, said that he was glad that I was going to join, and added appropriate words about the solemnity of the occasion, and what with his solemnity and my terror it was about as cheerful as an execution. However, I signed my name to the promise and the C.H. witnessed my signature. He wrote a good clear flowing hand, I remember. I was glad when the interview was over; and I must say I envied the C.H. to whom the Skipper spoke as to a trusted officer, almost as though he might ask his advice on some professional point; oh, to be in the position of the C.H., eminent in the ship, in fact, an officer in the ship.

Well, I did my best to keep my promise; most of the League's members did, I think; but like every other member I loathed the League's meetings; oh, those appalling meetings. Who among us would not have preferred to go down into the bilges and scrub out the limbers by hand?

I found one advantage in joining the League. The Captain of the Hold now knew me to be in some sort a shipmate, not only a new chum. He was not grim about my hammock after that evening, though I do not doubt that the bundle brought down by me for the first fortnight was clumsy enough to make him writhe. As to the League, we used to wonder how it had started. Though we did not know it, the suggester or prime mover sometimes came aboard to give us what we called a pi-jaw; ah, had some of the pirates among us known, or suspected. . . . Had he come aboard or gone off with any cutter's crew, it had been better for that man to have worn a diving suit.

All too quickly, the Saturday evening passed; there came eight bells with the pipe to clear up decks and petty officers to supper. Going down to fetch my broom, I passed the lighted door of what was called the forward hospital, and saw the godlike P.O.'s sitting to table, as though they had never been new chums. They had a messman to wait on them and a lobs-scouse to tuck into;

I envied them their ease, their certainty, their mastery of their fate.

I swept my deck, and as I swept was suddenly noticed by the Chief Officer, who said, "I don't think I have seen your face before, have I? How long have you been with us?"

"Two days, sir."

"It seems a bit strange, in the beginning. You'll soon get into it. This is your first ship, I expect."

"Yes, sir."

"She was mine, too, when I first went to sea. I was a midshipman on board. We had seven hundred and fifty men on board."

"Wherever did they sleep, sir?"

"We were packed just like sardines; and there was less room than now; the decks were full of guns."

Like every other man aboard, I felt great cheer from the presence of the Chief; he was much liked, and to be spoken to by him was counted an honour.

As I passed his cabin-door later, I had a glimpse of a bunk, a telescope on a rack, and one or two other things, a sword, and so forth, which again made me long for the time when I had so mastered this odd destiny as to have a place of my own. I was getting on, however; when I went for my hammock that night, it was something easier to find it. I now knew where to go, and had learned, that the quicker I could get it from the rack, the easier would it be to get it up the hatchway. I had, in fact, been smartened up a fraction.

135

New Chum

My first Sunday was not a very happy day. I had the usual unhappy search for a basin to wash in, found my hammock on the deck when I returned, and seemed no cleverer at lashing it than before. After breakfast, Dick said that we must make all our brass- and metal-work like the rising sun, for the Skipper and Chief would go round the whole ship, inspecting every little thing. We swept and swabbed our deck; we polished all the staunchions till they were like silver and all the rails and the capstan bands till they were like gold; then Dick told me to leave that, to make the falls and out-hauls tidy. These had to be "faked or flemished," he said, and at once showed me how to fake and to flemish. I enjoyed both processes, for even I, the beginner, could see that they added to our deck's appearance. All the ship's company was busy improving the ship's appearance. Our colours and the M.M.S.A. flag were hoisted; presently the sixteen-oared barge was manned, and sent in with a boat ensign flying, to fetch off the Chaplain. She looked very beautiful, I thought (but was not a pleasant boat to be in). When our deck was perfect, the pipe went for us to dress in our very best Sunday uniforms, so down we went, to change and smarten.

I was at my chest, changing. I was in shirt and trousers, engaged in blacking my shoes, when suddenly someone called to me to look out. With the tail of my eye, I saw a man kneeling down on the deck just behind me and close to. I had been sent down by one such before. I knew the symptoms; I was to be pushed on to him, fall over him, and then be punched by him for knocking him down, etc. At the same instant, a war-cry rang out, either Pile-ums, or Pile-o, perhaps both, and a gang of toughs, at least half a dozen strong charged in on me. I had had an instant's warning, and slipped to my right. My chest was amidships, my swerve brought me almost to the main hatch. The gang had hold of me, and were bent on a pile-ums (or pile-o), that is, they were going to roll in a pile on the deck with myself as the mattress: all good fun of course, to the rollers; painful to the watch below. You, who have seen a horse roll, will know with what abandon pilers rolled, and how good the process was for growing crops, or bodies, or uniforms. I was determined not to be the mattress. There was a lively scrum round the foot of the main hatch. One of the gang got me by the back of my collar, and gave it a strong wrench round:—

"Around the throat he knotted me . . .
In point of fact, garrotted me."

I was so nearly choked that I have no clear recollection of what happened, but I was told later that I had damaged one fellow's face, and that it was —— decent of him to take it as he did. The pile-ums did not take place, and the gang melted away. I went back to smarten up for divisions.

I had been almost choked, and did not feel very well. At the pipe, I went up to Divisions, and fell in. I was in a new suit, smelling of new cloth and stuffiness; I was standing at attention, dressed up to a seam, and kept at attention waiting for the Skipper and Chief, who were delayed by something, and were long in coming. I began to sway about, and asked Red Swab, if I might fall out. He said: "No; wait till they've been round. They'll be here in a tick." However, Dick saw my state, and plucked me out of the line and down the after hatch just as the Skipper came in. To the best of my knowledge, I fainted at the foot of the ladder. Dick very nimbly brought water from the Sick Bay, from the jug, and soon had me on my feet. We passed a few anxious minutes later, dodging the Skipper and Chief, going down to the orlop when they came down to the lower deck, and going up to the lower deck when they came down to the orlop. The Chief always wore a white glove upon one hand on Sunday mornings. As he went along the different decks, a white finger sometimes touched a beam or other cranny; if any dust came upon the finger, the P.O. responsible was called to account. But no man failed to be encouraged to do better when the Chief admonished him, he was the soul of goodness, kindness and courage. It was however the fact, that some of the men on board, like Huck Finn's father, could only have been civilised with a shot gun.

When the inspection was over, all hands sat for a while in what were called Bible Classes; school was rigged, and bringing our Bibles we read a little Genesis, with some comment from authority and a good deal of talk among ourselves; I felt very queer during Bible Class; and after Bible Class felt queer in Church.

Church was rigged on the after part of the main deck, just as Prayers had been, except that the harmonium was wheeled out from the Armoury, and more chairs were set for Officers and Masters. Most men came to Church with rugs for their ease. They folded these to sit upon, but if a new chum brought a rug, it was taken by an older hand. I had learned at Prayers what to expect at Church Service, and what I expected, I certainly received. It was impressive enough to be marched to our places, and to stand there while the ship's bell was solemnly tolled, and to see the port watch across the way, in four ranks, with the choir aft, near the harmonium. Then the Skipper's family entered; the Captain's wife went to the harmonium; the Skipper entered on the starboard side, the Chaplain came in by the port door, in his surplice, and instantly the service began. It was a time of torment for new chums. The little devils of mizentopmen were just behind us, with dwarfish ingenuity; just behind them were the foretopmen more resolute and more devilish than the lambies; and behind these, the robust maintopmen, who by making very long arms could hand implements of torture to those who could apply them. We were pinched, and pinned and prodded; once, as I sat after kneeling, I felt excruciating pain; I had sat upon a pin carefully and very skilfully bent. I had always been told, and had believed, that a prick from a pin often led to blood poisoning and death. Was I to die so young? And would blood poisoning contracted during Divine Service count as martyrdom, of a sort, and win me a golden crown? The kneeling and the sitting parts of the service were hard to bear. When we stood to sing, it was better; for the word had gone about that we were to make more noise than the port watch. I don't know whether we did, for they had the harmonium and the choir on their side; we only had the Skipper and a couple of Masters; still we did our best.

The hymns in use on board seemed to be chosen because they had good rousing tunes. With some popular numbers from the hymnal were some of the best from Moody & Sankey. I learned at once that the men behind me were shouting traditional parodies of the words. If the word Alleluia came in any hymns, the entire watch shouted: "Ally. Looly. Lums"; they seemed to get more weight on to the stretchers thus. . . . When we sang, "I am but a stranger here," they shouted:

> "P.O.'s and instructors stand
> Around me on every hand.
> I scrub the main deck forms with sand
> And I wish I were at home."

Whenever, by some chance the noise from the port watch seemed to be gaining upon us, the word was passed, that we filthy new chums were not singing. It was false; we were singing; but of course, they had the choir; and near the harmonium there was that giant of a man, the rumbustious man of the three who had questioned me. He had a topsail yard voice, which could out-bellow a tempest. We did our best; honours were about even.

I had expected martyrdom during the sermon, but the crown was denied me; something seemed to have caught the Captain's eye, and when he was in a noticing mood, the wickedest blood on board took cover. His eye was raking the starboard watch all through the sermon:

> "and O
> The difference to me."

Sunday dinner was always a feast; and the fact that I was not up to a feast made me welcome in a mess not so affected. After the feast, the ship's company for the most part pulled out desks and forms, so that they might spend the afternoon reading, writing letters, drawing, working at setting-in books, or other quiet amusement. I did as the others; I sat at a desk and wrote letters, listened to the chaff that passed among the wits, and longed more than I can say for the ease and certainty of bearing shown by the seniors. Footsteps passed overhead, where friends were mooching; it was a quiet time for all, except for an occasional boats' crew. Even the life of the River was quiet on Sundays.

Towards the end of the afternoon, the letters were made up; men went about asking for postage stamps, for not many were provided with these; then, the letters

141

were dropped in the box, and the mail master took them ashore to post them.

The Evening Service was much such an ordeal as the Morning Service had been. The hymns were somewhat better, and the singing rather noisier. For the first time, I heard the hymn "For those in peril on the sea", which was always a part of our Sunday Evening Service. We all soon learned the words by heart, and our singing of this hymn was a feat, and woe betide the new chum who didn't put his back into it. After Service there was mooching around, singing the indelicate old ditty; and then Sunday was over; it was time to clear up decks, and then go to Divisions for hammocks.

My trials were not over, even then. As I brought up my hammock, the clue of the hammock of the man in front of me upon the hatch untwisted from its tuck, and fell, as clues did. The heavy iron ring of the clue came with a blinding bang on to my eyebrow. I stopped from the sudden agony, and was punched by the man below me for blocking the gangway. "—— you," he said, "now you've been baptised. Perhaps you'll stand from under another time."

I did, thenceforward, stand from under; I was learning.

H.B. was at my slinging place. "Chum," he said, "you have been let down once or twice. You can't hitch your laniard properly. I'll show you how to hitch your laniard. It is very simple. Do this; then, do this; then, do this. There you have a hitch which no man can undo without waking you. Before you turn in at any time, just put your hand on the hitch; a touch will tell you if it has been altered. I never turn in, even now, without feeling the hitch."

He watched me pass the hitch for myself. "You see," he said, "that is secure. No one can undo that while you're turned in."

I felt that now I was secure. My heart glowed with gratitude to H.B. as I spun my choicest ghost yarns from many a Christmas number. At last, I fell asleep; but my bad Sunday was not yet over.

Some time in my deep sleep, there came upon me sudden violence, confusion, a struggle and then a painful bang, amid the noise of feet rushing away. I had been emptied right out of my hammock, with all my bedding on top of me. I was in some pain from the fall, but I hurried to replace my bedding and get back into my hammock. I knew well enough, that men were not allowed out of their hammocks without leave, and that if any officer had heard the thud of my body and came down to investigate, I, being out of my hammock, should be the one punished. I had been assured, that the punishment was to lash up the hammock and carry it for an hour.

Making a great effort on Monday morning, I got my hammock stowed and myself washed in such good time that I was able to go aloft alone before breakfast. I went up to the cross-trees, and again marvelled at the miracle of what I saw; a River full of ships of all sorts; two cities full of ships of all sorts; and far away mountains, blue and bold. In the docks on both sides were masts, sails, flags of ships in fifties and hundreds; above which the spars of one or two giants towered in a way that caught the eye. The big Cunarder had sailed on Saturday; her buoys were vacant still. Beyond those buoys, I saw again the white masts of the great ship which had caught my eye. Gulls were floating about, mewing; one or two of them perched on our main upper yards, with an effortless, silent power of exquisite grace. I knew nothing about the rigging yet. I divided it for myself, into two kinds, the one, safe to trust to, the other, very dangerous. After trees, which had been my only climbing, a mast seemed all romance, and height, and danger. This was a mast, a real mast, which had sailed the seas and been blown on by the hurricane.

I told myself that I would be aloft whenever I could, for as long as ever I could, that the delight would never pall, that I would soon run aloft, like those topmen on Friday. Glancing at the truck, so close to me, above my high perch, I thought, soon, soon, I will rest my chin upon you, look up, and see nothing whatever above me but sky.

Going aloft was a resource, when there was ample time, but in those early days, when I was sweeper and messman's assistant, as well as desperately anxious to learn, there were odd times of hanging about, waiting for the order, and making sure of being there when the order came. I could not understand the orders, remember. A shrill whistle blew, and someone shouted "yow, yow," or "yow, YOW," or "YOW, yow-yow." How was I to know what yow meant? How was I to yow, unless I could see my shipmates yowing? In fear of missing an order, I spent a lot of odd time, in those days on the lower deck, which was, after all, the focslemen's deck. On that deck, the Officer of the Day gave his orders to the P.O. of the deck, who gave them to his messenger, who gave them to the Instructor who piped and told men to yow. While I stayed there, I had a fourfold chance of learning what the order was.

There was nothing to do there, except wait, walk, keep out of the way, and read the Prize and Notice Boards. There was the Library, of course, but if any seniors of the tougher kinds were there, a new chum might as well have entered a lion's den. It was well to keep out of the way, for any seniors working on the lower deck, pumping or hauling, would impress a new chum if they could.

Even if I dodged these, the deck was dreary. I would lay aft, to look at the Prize Boards; then go over to port, to look at the gun; I would read its notice saying that water could be used for its slides where there was no fear of frost; then I would go forward to either bulkhead, to look at the framed questions in Seamanship, the Watch and Station Bills and an illustrated sheet showing how to restore Life to the Apparently Drowned.

All these dreary pastimes were mine in my first few

days. I was both bored and lost; yet even there I was jumped on, and made use of, sent to do something because I wasn't doing anything, or sent to do nothing because I was.

When I had been a few days aboard, I was reading how to restore life to the apparently drowned, near the Second Officer's cabin. I had often seen this Second Officer, but so far had had no dealings with him. He saw me, that I was new, and spoke. He was a big, burly, cheery sailor, very smart and well content. He seemed enormous to me. "Well, boy," he said, "what's your name?" I told him.

"Ah, yes," he said, and added my Christian names and address. I was pleased and startled, and said, "how did you know, sir?"

"Ah," he said, "not long since, I could tell the Christian names and addresses of every boy who has been here since I joined; now, I am not so sure. And how are you getting on?"

"Not very well, sir."

"How's that?"

"I find it very strange, sir."

"How long have you been on board?"

"Since Thursday, sir."

"Have you been punished yet?"

"No, sir."

"Boy," he said, "there are lots of men on board, who've been on board a year, or two years, or even more, and are being daily punished. You, who have

146

been here only since Thursday have not been punished at all. How can you say you're not getting on well? You're getting on very well. Only keep on as you've begun and you'll be a credit to us."

This was a word of cheer; my heart glowed within me at it; yet I saw the weakness of his position as clearly as the disadvantages of mine. I thanked him. He looked at me as a big friendly bear might look at a cub.

"Boy," he said, "come to my cabin door a moment."

This was just round the corner from where we stood. I went to the door, and gazed in at that marvellous place, an officer's cabin, with everything handsome about it. He went to the table, set out for his meal and took from it a little pot. "Boy," he said, "can you eat jam?"

"Yes, sir."

"Well, take this pot; and remember this, no boy is not doing well who can eat jam."

I thanked him again, and took the pot. It was one of the little sample pots sent by jam makers to possible purchasers. This officer, as ship's caterer, and excellent, beyond all praise, in that office, doubtless received many such. I had never before seen a sample pot; it seemed like a little jewel, and to have a little jewel delightful to eat approached felicity. I saved it till tea, then took it to the mess, and shared it with my friend.

The hours dragged queerly by. I liked my Master; he seemed to think that I was interested in some subjects and eager to know them; I liked the officers, Skipper,

Chief and Second, and dreaded lest I should displease them. I liked many of the men on board already; there were many first-rate men there, but then, of course, there were others, and always there was this cramped odd life between decks, this smell of paint and tar, this rush, tumult and order, an utter absence of privacy of any kind, the impossibility of so much, and the strangeness of everything. I have never felt so lost, so uprooted, so without foothold.

Early in my first full week on board, soon after dinner, we were piped to a 'Muster by Open List' on the main deck. This practise continued once a week throughout my time aboard. We never knew what purpose it served, nor can I imagine that it served any, for each one of us was observed at mess thrice and at Divisions twice in every twenty-four hours. Still, there it was, we fell in; an Officer had a look at us, the Gunner sat at a table with the muster book, read each name in turn, and as each man was called, he had to answer, pass bare-headed past the Officer and so away. The ceremony had this that was unusual in it. The names were called by terms, in alphabetical order. The usual period on board was two years; a few men, for some reason or another, stayed an extra term or two; a very few men stayed a whole three years. The ceremony, being new to me, impressed me; and what impressed me more, was the appearance of the oldest hands, the fossils and survivors of buried and forgotten years. The first half dozen, shall we say, were all men of more than two years' service. I shall never forget the appearance of those old hands. One or two of them were of course P.O.'s; those were not the ones to be marked. The men who took the eye were the old salts, who would never be promoted, whose boast was, that they were men of the people, the stock that remained, while dynasties and creeds went by. It is hard to describe them; they were tough, they were salted, they were weather-beaten. They walked in a way of their own; they wore their (always rather battered) uniforms with a slovenliness of their own. As I looked at these old hands, I sometimes saw them remove their tobacco quids before their names were called, and replace them after they had passed the Officer. I soon came to know the muster by heart, and thereby the term of each man aboard. Being a new chum, my own name came very late in the list; I had time to observe the ship's company, to learn the names and judge the natures.

I have told of my joy in being aloft. That heart would have been dead indeed who could not find beauty in the River. At all seasons, at all states, the River was beautiful. At dead low water, when great sandbanks were laid bare, to draw multitudes of gulls; in calm, when the ships stood still above their shadows; in storm, when the ferries beat by, shipping sprays, and at full flood when shipping put out and came in, the River was a wonder to me. Sometimes, as I sat aloft in the cross-trees, in those early days, I thought how marvellous it was, to have this ever-changing miracle about me, with

mountains, smoky, glittering cities, the clang of ham-
mers, the roar and hoot of sirens; the miles of docks, the
ships and attendant ships, all there for me, seemingly
only noticed by me, everybody else seemed to be used to
it by this time, or to have other things to do.

I went aloft, whenever I had the chance; I practised
trotting aloft, in the way of the topmen at sail drill, and
had some sudden scrapes on my shin from missing the
ratline as I trotted.

All the time, I was longing for Wednesday, when the
juniors would go to the Baths. The Baths were an exquisite memory; that green, clear salt water was enough
to lure any boy, and then, to reach them, the boy would
have to voyage in a steam ferry, with either a screw or a
pair of paddles, steered by a man at the wheel, past,
and often very close to, ships of strange beauty and interest, about which my shipmates always seemed to
know everything. Then, at the threshold of the Baths
were docks, with ships in them. Going to the Baths, in
itself was intense pleasure, had all these other joys attendant on it.

When the day came, one of my fellow focslemen
warned me that I should be jolly well ducked at the
Baths. I had already heard this, that new chums were
ducked "the first time". I was not much alarmed at the
news; I expected to be ducked. What was being ducked,
to one who could swim? You went under, and then
came up; it would be nothing more than baptism to one
of riper years. Who could mind a ducking? It crossed

my mind that the man who warned me must be rather an ass to mind a little ducking more or less. What had he come to sea for, if not to be soused in salt water? Besides, as I thought, none but juniors would be at the Baths with me, and all the toughs of the ship, so far as I could know were seniors.

After dinner on the day, there came the order 'Seniors to the Field. Juniors to the Baths. Clear up decks. Dismiss.' I was all smartened up for the shore; and found, to my joy, that we were all to be carried directly to the pier at New Ferry in the steam launch, and should therefore run no risk of being caught for pony racing along the Esplanade. I was somewhat dashed to find that the launch was crammed with seniors, all the seniors, all the toughs, all the pirates. They had somehow won leave to come to the Baths, although it was juniors' day. I had not reckoned upon this, and felt the iniquity of the injustice that gave so much to seniority and so little to the deserving poor. However, there they were, and as usual, they made us know it. In the launch, they packed us down in the cabin, till it was like the Black Hole in Calcutta. In the ferry steamer, they sent us forward, so that we could be out of sight of them. I enjoyed the River journey none the less, and already took in some of the points; such a ship was the . . . of such a line; such another the famous . . . ; those moorings, the regular berth of a line known all over the world. There was the famous *Skirmisher;* those odd-looking tugs were the well-known queens of the tug world, each a heroine of adventure. As we came nearer to the Stage, some of the seniors moved forward among us, to look towards Woodside. I found that they were looking at the lofty white spars which had caught my eyes a few days before. The ship was still there; these seniors said that she was the *Wanderer,* and that she was by much the finest ship now in dock. I liked the name, the *Wanderer.* It struck into my mind as a name of beauty, as a sort of seagull of grace there. The *Wanderer* . . . the more I thought of the name, the more wonderful it seemed. It suggested skies of desolation, with a planet; seas of loneliness, with that ship in sail. She was to sail soon, they said; the question rose, whether we should have a Liverpool Leave, that is, a whole holiday, with leave to go where we liked in Liverpool, before we sailed. If we did, seniors said, that she was the ship they would first make for.

As we drew in, to the Stage, these seniors took place close to the gangway, so that they might be the first people ashore. I did not understand their eagerness till a fellow focsleman said that it was "to get a good start". They would leap ashore the instant the gangway fell, and race to the Baths' entrance (a hundred yards or so from the Stage) so that they might seize and claim some favoured undressing rooms for themselves and their friends. They also had private bets among themselves, as to which should be first undressed and in the water. All the ship's company loved swimming above all

earthly pastimes; even one little extra half minute in
that exquisite green salt water was well worth the strug-
gling for. As the gangway fell, the crowd of men
charged for the Baths. I charged with them, that is, after
them, with the men of my own term. When we reached
the Baths, we found that the seniors had occupied all
the rooms near the deep end, and stood at the doors of
them to flick us with towels to the rooms at the shallow
end, the fitting place for filthy chums. The rooms were
equally good at the shallow end.

Though I had not yet the ship's speed in flinging off
my clothes, the sight of that salt water made me hurry.
Along the sides of the Baths were metal mouths ever
spouting more green water; at the shallow end were
gratings through which the surplus gurgled away. The
baths were filled with the splash of falling fountains,
the happy noise of water, startled every instant by a
warning cry, followed by the wash of a plunge, as some
great diver went in from the high board. The sound
alone always told if the dive had been a good one. The
Baths were a little small; that was their one defect;
small, that is, for two-thirds of our ship's company. Still,
I suppose that no hours in our boyhood compared for
one instant with the hours spent in that clear green
splashing pool. How the salt water was obtained, made
clear and green, and ever renewed, were miracles of
skill about which we did not bother; our aim was to get
into it as soon as possible and to stay in it till we were
ordered out; unless, that is, we had designs on "Simp-

sons' ", the famous tea-shop on the Stage. I was soon in
the water, as happy as a boy can well be. The thought
of ducking never entered my head; and indeed, I began
to think that it was a false alarm. All my fellow focslemen kept in the shallow end; the seniors alone ruled
the deep end, with its spring-boards and high dives.
From time to time, a shout from the deep end warned
us to keep the end clear, while some of the great divers
competed in diving together, and getting to the shallow
end and back under water.

The reader may think that the focslemen were silly
sheep to endure these tyrannies. "Surely," he will ex-
claim, "a little resolute concerted action would have
quelled these assumptions of the seniors; what spiritless
outcasts these new chums must have been." There were
about forty of us new chums. Present at the Baths that
day there may have been a hundred who were not new
chums, and perhaps fifty of these, strictly speaking,
were juniors still. Could not these fifty have banded
with our forty into a ninety, and the ninety, gathered
together, have suppressed the fifty seniors? Yes, no
doubt, if they *had* gathered together, but this was the
one thing made impossible by the system of loyalties
which ruled the ship. Those fifty juniors were all members of tops. All the seniors, without exception, were, or
had been, members of those tops, and to turn upon a
fellow topman, past or present, was a deed of infamy
unthinkable; it was not done. To join the fifty seniors
in some real raid upon the new chums, to put them

finally in their place, that those fifty juniors would gladly do; but to join new chums against topmen, would be anarchy; schoolboys might do a thing like that, never topmen.

In spite of the seniors, I had a happy swim, and having begun to feel somewhat cold, as we all did, after a time, in the water, was thinking of coming out and dressing. I was on my way to the steps, when an exceedingly high-spirited, red-haired senior whose name I forget, but whose exulting face I shall ever remember, swam suddenly up, caught me by the scruff, and cried: "Go down, chum," and suddenly thrust me under. I was caught unawares, I had my mouth open, and as I went down I took a mouthful of salt water, which made me cough as I came up. As I sputtered, a big ruffian, a terrible fellow, thrust me down a second time, very violently, and held me down. I know that I struggled, and came up, but others were waiting for a share of the fun, and had it. I am not at all clear about some of the rest of the swim. I know that for a time it was exceedingly unpleasant, and then became like a bright cornfield. I heard a rush of feet, a strong arm plucked me violently out of the water, and I heard the fierce voice of William Tozer who had pulled me out asking indignantly: "Do you want to drown the boy?" In some way, quite unknown to myself, I had been handled transversely right across the Baths. I had been sent under near the N.W. shallow end, and was pulled out at the S.E. deep end. A very little more would have made me Apparently

Drowned but that would not have mattered much among so many who had a rough knowledge of how to deal with such cases. I went to my dressing-room by the land route; enough of water had I, for that moment of time.

Being dressed, and now free of the Baths, for men said I shouldn't be ducked again (and, indeed, I never was), I went to the Stage, where, with some misgivings, not knowing how a new chum might be greeted, I went into Simpsons. It was like most refreshment rooms. It had a counter with glass cases full of cakes; and a number of little tea tables and chairs. The seniors had already taken the tables and were uproarious together there, with all the fun and jokes from which we were separated. I went to the counter for one or other of the dainties offered. In summer, these were ices; at other seasons, Eccles cakes, parkins and rock cakes. On the wall, behind the counter, was a big oil painting of the River, as it showed between 1865 and '75, when steamers were small and topsails single; this, the marine artists among us used to stare at with admiration and envy; ah, to be able to paint the moving water and the rippling sail like that.

Usually, we had some little time in Simpsons. Some men slipped away for quiet smokes further along the Stage; a man told me, that if I wanted anything to read, I had better buy it at the bookstall nearby; many men bought reading matter there, either for themselves, or for friends on board.

When we were back at New Ferry, getting into our ship's boats, H.B. appeared. He had not been at the Baths, but upon some ship's mission into Liverpool (to buy a new hygrometer, if I remember rightly). He caught hold of me and shoved me down alongside him in the stern-sheets of a cutter. "Come on and sit by me," he said. "Make room for him, will you? This chum," he explained, "knows all the ghost yarns that ever were written."

"He was —— near made a ghost himself this afternoon," somebody said, and there was a general laugh.

We were in the port stern-sheets of our cutter. Like all liberty boats, she was crammed fore and aft, with every oar double banked, and possibly fifteen or twenty other men packed in somehow. It was a maintop crew, very smart, and with each oar double banked she travelled. Now, being rowed in a boat was a new delight, and nothing approaching boat sense had yet been knocked into me. I blush to say, that as we sped up to the gangway, with the port oars tossed, and the bowman standing up to catch his turn, my left hand was over the cutter's gunwale. In one instant more, it would have ground between the cutter and the gangway, and with the way we carried and the weight we bore it would have been made a very poor collection of fingers. Just at the instant, H.B. saw it, and snatched my arm to safety. "Oh, chum, chum," he said, "you must never do that again; never, never, never." Indeed, on the instant the place where my hand had lain ground against the gangway, in a way which made my blood run cold. "You see?" H. B. said, "where would your hand have been, eh?" I did see. I had liked H.B. before that, as a quite extraordinarily nice fellow; now he had saved me from a very nasty knock, and I knew not how to thank nor praise him.

Of course, he was a super senior, the most popular man in the ship, and wearing the halo of "waiting for orders to join". I could not expect him to notice a new chum, to the point of walking with him; I never did walk with him. I had the privilege of spinning ghost yarns to him, and this was very much to me. Oh, what pains I took with them, knowing that he liked them. In my first weeks on board, he did more than anybody to make me glad that I was there. I used to watch him in the mornings as I polished my staunchions while he superintended the cleaning of the B.L. Vavasour gun. Once, seeing my interest, he called me over, let me open the marvellously fitting breech, slide in the projectile, shut the breech piece to; then, open up and unload. Often, in wet weather, in those early days, as I wandered lost, looking now at the Watch and Station Bills; then at the seamanship questions, then at the methods of restoring Life to the Apparently Drowned, then laying aft to the door of the library, but not quite daring to go in, from the roar of the pirates within, the thought of H.B. was an ample amend for everything. When I walked with any of the half dozen with whom I soon had the habit of walking, the talk, as was the way with new chums, ran always upon the topic, of who was a terror and who was a decent chap. Seven or eight men on board were certainly terrors; their deeds and words were repeated with horror. When we turned to praising the good, I could say, "I'll tell you who is a most awfully decent chap: H.B." Then, to my delight, my fellow would say: "Yes, easily the decentest chap on board, and the cleverest. But he'll get his orders any day now; and I don't know who'll be the decentest chap, then. What would you say to so-and-so?" Alas, the thought that H.B. would soon be gone sent a pang through me; I felt that nobody very decent would be left, except perhaps Dick. He was a decent chap, but not in the same solar system with H.B.; kind, yes, decent, and a good seaman. Still, quality, style, those were the things; H.B. had style; Dick only goodness and talent.

The days passed with a slow growth in each. I came to understand that the ship swung always head to tide; that you could tell "slack water" by the look, and that when we swung to the flood or ebb, we were only swinging, not broken adrift. I learned, roughly, whereabouts the ropes were, which I was expected to haul upon at sail or spar drills, and, roughly, what purposes they served. I learned also the simple knots, bends and hitches; the names of many parts and bits of the ship; and all the routine of every day. I began to understand what the different pipes meant, and to learn the unpleasantness of three different kinds of pumps. The big Downton pumps I had been broken into in my first evening. Soon, I had the knowledge of the bilge pump; a wheeled contrivance, with brakes which Dick showed me how to rig, and washers which Dick showed me how to fit, and spells which Red Swab made me heave round at, three or four of us focslemen manning each brake at a time. Like most wooden ships, ours leaked a little; sometimes, more than a little; the well was sounded daily. Presently, as we drew the decaying water forth, I learned what was meant by the "smell of bilge water". Dick used to put on sea boots just before the appalling stench broke forth; he disappeared down into the hold, "to broom out the bilges". I used to envy him the job, down there at the very bottom of an old man-of-war. Later, just before the ship was docked for repairs, when I had to do that job myself sometimes twice a day, on very bad days thrice, I was not the gladder for it. But much as I loathed the bilge pump, it was at least done in concert; it was a delight compared with the fresh-water pump, at which one hove alone, twenty or thirty strokes to the spell.

Our fresh water came off in "the Water Boat" and was pumped by the launch's engine into tanks in the hold, from which each mess in turn pumped it up to half a dozen other tanks for daily uses. As there were about fourteen messes, the duty fell about once a fort-night: as a couple of hundred men use a good deal of water daily the task was not light. If our mess had to pump fresh water on a day when the bilges were bad (say, a foot, and I sometimes found them more than a foot), we had as much pumping as we could manage. The fresh-water pump was very stiff to work.

We had in our focsle a very powerful young man who enjoyed showing his strength on it. He would put in a matchless spell of the usual length, to show us how it should be done. Then Dick or Red Swab would say: "There, you see how to do it. Now let's see you do it properly for once. Heave round, now." However, little boys of thirteen cannot do the feats performed by big boys of sixteen. Later, I came to know how Dick and Red Swab must have suffered, while the pump handle slowly rose and fell and the water trickled into the tank above. Sometimes they would go up to the tank to see how it was getting along; they would come down with long faces, saying: "The water is only dripping in. You'll be all night here at this rate. Come on, now, try if two of you cannot do it." Then a second little boy would catch hold of the handle, and some slight improvement would show for a little while.

Later, when we little ones had grown a lot, we learned the knack of pumping, of using our weight and keeping to a rhythm. Probably, all of us, before we left the ship, could pump for half an hour without fatigue, single-handed.

I was eager to begin well, and to please Dick and Red Swab. I did my best at all my work, and my very best at the work which I enjoyed most. This was the polishing of brass rails and steel staunchions every morning of term.

My first sea delight was undoubtedly first tasted on the lower deck, when I found that I could make my steel staunchions brighter than any staunchions on the deck. There was a way of moving the emery paper horizontally, which made the steel like mirrors (or like the silver paper round chocolates). All the Brother Lawrences in the cloister (the poor saps) moved their emery paper vertically, which gave a dismal effect, like the lead foil round tea or tobacco. My staunchions were praised, and I was promoted to the brass rail in front of the Prize Board, which I found yielded to the same method, and could be made like pure gold. The port watch did their brass with the filthy mess known as Gumption. Dick urged me to use Gumption, till I showed him that the use of Gumption is fatal to any lasting shine. Gumption is made of brick-dust and oil. I never used oil; ask me not what I used; the result was glorious. It was a piece of work which I could do with my whole heart and do well; "better than it had ever been done before," Dick said. This piece of praise was almost the first thing which made me feel that I had a place on board.

I mentioned the two old main-deck twenty-four-pounder muzzle-loading cannon which used to stand between the cables on the lower deck. I examined these with deep interest. There were old men on board who had worked guns of just that sort. They told me how they had been aimed, by handspikes, quoins and tackles; they told me the names of the different parts. I noticed, that each gun had a sight on a reinforce. While examining the sight on our starboard gun, I found that it was of brass, which had been blacked over. With a little rubbing, I got the blacking away, and polished the brass beneath. It became like the crest of a golden-crested wren.

Then, as I went to work on it in the morning, I found more brasswork under the blacking; the mounts for the locks and the sights were of brass of a peculiarly beautiful quality which took a deeper glow than other brass. Dick was doubtful about letting me polish these, "they never had been done before; the port watch might kick at having to polish theirs, if we did ours; it didn't pay to be ambi". However, I pleaded to be allowed to do them and Dick judged, that no officer would be likely to see both guns at once, the one glowing and the other gloomy; he let me clean them. I found that the soft dark stuff of our working caps was the best natural polisher of brass; no other rag could compare with it. I made those brass fittings to glow each morning. All through that term they glowed. When I returned on board after the holidays, no longer a new chum, they glowed no more. Someone, in reblacking the guns, had blacked over the brass. It gave me a pang, though I was no longer working the lower deck, and never again had a hand in cleaning its bright-work.

In all my spare time, if the weather were fair, I went aloft, to the foretopmast cross-trees. For some days, I found the bunt of the foretopgallant yard a favourite seat; then, as I sat there one afternoon, the ship's terror hailed me from the deck, and bade me get off that yard. "What are you doing on the bunt of that sail?" he shouted. "Do you suppose we furled that bunt for a filthy chum to sit on? Get off it, or we'll skin you alive."

In sail drill, our sails were furled Navy fashion, with a wrinkleless cone of sail, crossed with broad black plaited gaskets, in the very centre of the yard. This cone, the bunt, in its wrinkleless perfection, or skin, was not easy to form. Topmen took great pride and often spent a long time in making it perfect. After drill, they would look at their work with comment. The main would say: "A nice furl. but look at the thing the —— fore have got. See it? Well, I ask you." The fore would say: "A —— nice bunt if you ask me. But, do look at what the main call a furl," etc.

I got off the yard as I was bidden, and sat there no more; I kept to the cross-trees; no one minded who sat in the cross-trees. As the days grew colder, fewer chums came aloft with me, and none but new chums came so far. I had quickly found that most of our crew were bored with the ship's routine. They did smartly what they had to do, nothing more. I found, too, that many men had telescopes or binoculars, which they almost never used after their second terms. They (or the juniors among them) always gladly lent these. I used to borrow a glass before going aloft

"And lo, Creation widened in my view."

With a glass, I could watch the shipping in the River close to us and the working of the crews about decks. There was nearly always some ship at anchor near us; usually a Norwegian barque, a Greek brig; or something small of our own. Sometimes listed steamers lay there. Beyond them, I could see men at work on the frames on the slips at Potters' Yard, or the riveters at Lairds'. I could see the little crowds at dock gates, waiting to cheer a ship away; the smoke of the tug, plucking the beflagged ship through. I could see Pier Head waving caps as the ship passed into the stream, and then an instant or two later would hear the cheering, and the answer of the ship's crew. After rain I used to watch slow old seamen, watchmen and ship's husbands, painfully loosing all sails, so that they might dry. Possibly thirty ships, some of them queens, would have their sails lifting and shining all day long. It was a lovely sight, even at that distance; I longed to be nearer to them. I could see that these ships were not rigged as ours, and the question rose: "Can it be as easy to go aloft in those, as it is here?"

I asked H.B. about it one night. He said: "Always once or twice a term there is a Liverpool Leave; and anyone can go to Liverpool. Most people go to the Baths for as long as they can stand it, but everybody goes round the docks to look at the ships. We always go aboard any fine ship, and ask if we can go aloft; the mate is usually on deck somewhere; no one ever refuses. It's a very different thing from going aloft here, of course.

Many of the ships are very lofty. The quantity of gear and the size of the yards are simply terrifying. Go aloft in as many of these ships as you can. It stretches your legs, I can tell you. You come down feeling that you've ridden twenty miles on a cart horse. Remember, you *must* do this; it's your only chance of learning any modern rigging whatever. Always choose the biggest and the newest ships; then you may learn what you'll find later."

I remembered this advice, and acted on it, later; in the meantime I stared at the ships; and judged, that the biggest and newest of them were terrifying as H.B. said.

One day, a big full-rigged ship anchored in the Sloyne, not far from us. Old hands said, that she was the . . . , and that old . . . was in her. I did not know enough to be interested in the ship, and old . . . . was unknown to me, having left before my time. However, very soon, old . . . put off from his clipper in a little dock skiff, pulled alongside us, and came aboard. I was told that he had been a kind of H.B. in his day, so I looked at him with awe. He looked tough and tanned as first voyagers usually did; "afterwards" it was said, "they all looked starved". He wore "serges", that is, dark blue reefer clothes, with black buttons; and had a gold chinstay round his cap badge. He was looked at with envy by all hands; here was the butterfly; we were but grubs. He came down to the orlop deck, close to where my chest stood; he even spoke to me; but when I met him the next time, forty years later, he had forgotten this. New chums were born to be forgotten anyway.

The ship's year was divided into two Halves; September to Christmas; February to July. These Halves were subdivided roughly in October and at Easter. We had no regular holidays at either half-term; no leave of any kind in October, and an odd suspension at Easter, at which some had leave to go home; others went with the officers on some expedition or semi-camp in Wales or the Wirral. For some reason, not clear to us, many men joined the ship for the first time at these half-terms, which certainly they would never have done, if they had only known. They were "October Boys" and "Easter Boys"; that is, younger hands than the bulk of the new chums, who came at the beginning of the half.

I had not been many weeks on board, when the October Boys joined us. Before this happened, their names appeared in the Watch and Station Bills; we read the odd names, and wondered what sort of chaps they would be. Men who for one reason or another had had to go to the outfitters at the Sailors' Home, returned with news that their chests were there. Then in an afternoon, men and chests came aboard up the gangway; and, lo, automatically, without merit, without effort, without possible question or criticism, I was exalted, shoved upwards, no longer the youngest hand aboard; I was senior to all these new chums. I could see with my own eyes, how repulsive the new chum really was. Could it be that I had looked like these, with my cap jammed over my eyes, a doddering walk, calling everybody "sir", and asking what the man with the whistle had said? Surely, I had never been as these? Surely, some sort of native grace had touched me? Red Swab was pointed about it. "Now you can see what you were; and now you can jolly well turn to, and help to lick them into shape; I'm not going to break in a second lot of colts; no thank you." Well; we had lively memories of our first days aboard; we did our best by these poor creatures; after all, it was not wholly their fault.

Very suddenly, H.B.'s orders came through; he was to leave at once, have a day or two at home, then proceed to his ship, thousands of miles away. I had known from the first that this would happen; all the same, the news laid me low. H.B. would be gone on the morrow, what would the ship be like without him? I had been a grubby little new chum, yet he had let me spin him ghost yarns. He had saved my hand from a nasty crush. He had been kind and wise and friendly; and now he was going, and tomorrow night he would not sling next me, and ask for a really good ghost. He, of course, as I could see, was happy about it. He was leaving the ship, going home, and bound for far away; all jolly things. All his friends, the seniors, were making the most of his last hours; I could not get near him. I hung about at a distance and saw him there, never with less than three about him. I hoped to catch him going to the P.O.'s supper, but he was supping with the Skipper, and did not appear. I thought I might see him bring his hammock; even this, he did not do. His second

brought and slung his hammock, and said that H.B.
wouldn't be down till about midnight, as he was saying good-bye to all the Masters, and then to all the
main. Well, of course, they had all known him for years.
I made ready the best ghost stories still in my collection, in case he might like them. He came down to his
hammock very late; almost everybody was asleep. He
was sad as he undressed. "It's sad, saying all these good-
byes," he said. I knew only too well how sad. I asked if
he would like a yarn. He said: "No, thanks very much;
it's very late, now. We should wake the sleepers, and
that's what sailors must not do. Good night." He shook
hands, and rolled himself up.

Well. We have to learn, that the fatal morning
comes; the next morning came, as it had to come, with
the rush to get things done; no chance of a word with
H.B. He was leaving the ship before half-past seven,
in order to catch his train, and therefore had a privileged breakfast somewhere. His third lashed up and
stowed his hammock; it was gone when I came down;
H.B. was gone; his chest was gone. The sight of the gap
in the line of chests, where his chest had lain, almost
broke my heart. We went to the main deck for Tables.
When we had set them, we were piped on deck to cheer
ship. I never really said good-bye to H.B. He was on
the lower deck, then, at the gangway, saying good-bye
to Officers and Masters; I was with the focsle and foretopmen in the starboard fore rigging and hammock

nettings. All hands had gathered there, to see H.B. go down the gangway into the steam launch, where his lashed chest stood. The gangway was full of Officers, saying good-bye. He went into the launch, which shoved off, went ahead a few revs, ported a spoke or two, and lay by. As she lay there, the singer, who drew so cleverly, an old messmate of H.B. shouted out: "Your spare butter, H.B." Who but a vulgarian and a miscreant, could talk or think of butter when he ought to have been broken-hearted? The Officer of the Day, down in the gangway, called out: "H.B. is now leaving us. Let us wish him all success and happiness. Three cheers for H.B." We could always cheer, broken-hearted or not; few young men could make more noise than we. We cheered, while H.B. stood at attention, bare-headed. Then the launch skipper cried: "Shove ahead"; the screw thrashed and the launch sped away with her dwindling figures; we were piped down to breakfast; a mockery of a meal it was to me.

I asked Red Swab, if I might put my chest where H.B.'s had stood. He said: "Yes, if nobody else has bagged the place. Your chest ought not to be where it is now." Immediately after breakfast, I ran down, and shifted my chest. Why nobody had bagged the place, I never could understand, for it was just under a port, and therefore perfect for reading; besides, it was hallowed; H.B.'s chest had lain there.

Nothing in my boyhood hurt me so cruelly as the loss of H.B. He was adored by all hands hardly less than

by myself. One of the cruel things about his going was
that

> "in a few days, everyone
> Went on his way, as if he had not been."

It was not so with me.

What became of him? All through that term, I hoped
that perhaps he might send me a postcard, or something, which I could treasure forever, some word or
tiny scrap of writing; even a message. He did not; and
I explained this to myself by the knowledge, that he
was now a new chum himself, on the other side of the
world, with plenty of things to occupy him and put me
out of mind. He wrote to the Chief, of course; for I
asked the Chief about him, and had the joy of hearing
that he was doing very well, "of course, he is sure to do
very well". For many years I contrived to follow his
career; then, this ceased to be possible. I know not what
became of him; but I have thought of him every day
for more than half a century. Surely, I was the luckiest
of all new chums, to have such a man to sling next to at
my first coming aboard.

During my first day on board, as I have said, a young
man called me "a —— orphan". The expression had not
pleased me at the time, but it now came in very handily.
I was told that, from time to time, certain of the toughs
of the ship held a concert, at which new chums and
unpopular men were made to sing. The concerts were
not held from any love of song, far from it. They were

held to gratify cruelty; the wish was to beat someone with a rope's end, a teaser or a belt; certainly, for not singing, and probably, for not singing well enough, but anyhow, for something. Usually, the excuse for beating could be found. Now and then, of course, the singers so charmed the court that they voted acquittal. "Orpheus with his lute made trees."

I had been warned that I should probably be made to sing before I had been many days aboard; and the warning scared me, for I had only two songs, and was dim about the tune of one and the words of the other; "snatches of old song" I had in abundance; not enough, I feared, to act as neck-verse.

One evening, as I came down to my chest for something, a press-gang of four or five suddenly closed in on me and seized me. "We want you," they said. "Come on, now; you've got to sing, my buck." I saw, then, that the starboard fore was crowded; a concert was in progress. I was pretty well scared when I saw the toughs who were acting as judges and executioners; they were the terrors of the ship. However, there was no drawing back; the thing had to be faced. I was flung by the press-gang into the circle; one of the judges told me to stand on that chest and sing. I was about to try my luck, when a man called out: "No, no, not that chum; he's a —— orphan."

"All right," the judges said, "top your boom, orphan. Get out of the fore. Let's have someone else."

They did not have anyone else, as it happened, for

hands were piped for something; and the victim escaped. In spite of the warnings given to me, there was only one other concert during my time aboard; this was in my second Half, when I was still a junior. I was caught by the press-gang as before, and kept with other victims ready for trial by the same judges and executioners. Hands were piped to something or other before my turn came, so my music never had a chance upon those truly savage breasts.

The young are frequently ingeniously cruel; the men who arranged these concerts knew very well, that most little boys suffer from stage fright. They knew, that many of their victims would be overcome by stage fright, so that they would fail to sing, and could then be ropes-ended, just to teach them. I judge, that before my time concerts may have been frequent on board; there were none in my last year. I do not doubt, that some other devilry was devised, to teach these filthy chums not to be so —— uppish; new chums asked for it, anyway; besides what were they there for, if not to be put through it?

After I had been two or three weeks aboard, and had had most of my being, inside and out, —— by somebody for something or other, I suddenly found myself less ——. There must have been very little of the fabric that hadn't been done, but the change was grateful, and was marked, moreover, by a sudden friendship, which lasted for a year. The reader may remember the mention of a pirate who had —— my blood and much else, first, on passing him in the port mizen with my hammock, and again, in going to a mess with Red Swab's plate? I had formed the notion that this pirate was little better than a child of Belial. Mark, now, how wrong I was.

Suddenly, one morning in the break, when going to my chest for something, this man hailed me with "Chum; just half a minute". I halted, and in the friendliest possible way he took my arm and started to mooch. He said: "Did your Mother come from . . . ?" I said: "Yes." "Well," he said, "I've had a letter from *my* Mother. She knew your Mother very well, and asks me to keep an eye on you. I come from those parts myself."

We began to talk of "those parts", some of which I knew a little. In those days, the safety bicycle was only just beginning, and boys had not so great a range as they have today. We had but touched the extreme verges of each other's country; still, we knew the main landmarks, and found this a bond. He was a man with a great knowledge of country things, as well as a sure instinct for the sea. I daresay he —— a few new chums when provoked beyond human endurance; as a friend, he was interesting and delightful. Certainly, as a friend, I never heard him swear. He went by the name of Hob; he told me, that everybody called him "Hob", and that of course I must. We both had lively memories of floods on the Avon. His wish was for a rousing flood in the winter holidays, so that he might build a raft, embark,

and see if he could reach the Severn. This was the sort
of thing I most longed to do; we talked of it for hours,
and for many many days to come. We became real
friends, but there was, of course, always a sort of gulf,
of a year of seniority between us. He laid me under
many obligations; my memories of the ship are much
mixed with him. He was a good, steady practical seaman, very reliable and thorough, if not very smart or
clever. He did well at sea, of course, and died at sea,
many years ago. What we longed to do in some summer
holidays was to build a raft like the one in *Huckleberry
Finn,* with steering sweeps and a wigwam, to embark
below the last weir, and drift as far as we could get,
living on a ham, a cheese, and a sack of ship's biscuits,
till we fetched up, say, at Newport, Mon., where we
could sell the raft for firewood, and take the train home
on the proceeds. However, he went to sea in the summer holidays; the raft was never more than a dream.

I had by this time done a good deal of pumping on
the Downton brake pumps; and suggested to Hob, that
our raft, in addition to steering sweeps, should have
something like a light Downton pump, properly oiled
and geared, which, when fitted with small paddle-wheels
on each side, would give to our saucy craft the impul-
sion, say, of four or five oars on a broadside without
wearing out the crew. Like the practical seaman he was,
he leaped at this notion, and felt sure it would work,
but better in a boat, he thought, with a pair of brakes

. . . and then . . . there were no such things at present . . . they would have to be made, and made after the raft. . . . We had to discuss many problems in the fitting of these paddles, which are not fitted yet.

Half the couples mooching the decks with us were discussing problems of the sort, all connected with water transport during the holidays. We were always talking of the holidays, and of the watery feats we hoped to do in them, and seldom did. One or two main-topmen were looked up to with awe, because they had arranged to go in a Runcorn topsail schooner to one of the Irish ports; they did it, too, and chewed tobacco the next term with an air of the Roaring Forties.

I find, that I have not been able to tell the effect which the ship had made upon me. It was profound; it was translation to another world utterly unlike anything before known, read of, or imagined. I had been plucked up by the roots and pitched endways, to strike root or die; now the roots were trying to catch something.

I had been very fond of stories of all kinds, and had read and invented many; with some thought, even, that some day, I might write stories. My coming to the ship put what I now called "a stopper over all" upon any such thought. Stories, reading and invention were shut suddenly away. I had to learn a new language and a new life, word by word, task by task; my past was dead; my present, not made.

Eyes were on me, all the time; judging eyes, which divided me up into good and bad columns, in the manner of Defoe. Thus, my focsle captains might say:

GOOD

He does his staunchions and brass-work well.
He sweeps honestly, and doesn't try to hide the dust in odd corners.
He isn't as hopeless with his hammock as he was.
We don't have to tell him again and again.

But, then, BAD

He is a rotten fresh-water pumper.
He is no good on the bilge pump.
He lost us half our butter, that time.
He doesn't even know the tucks of an eye-splice, yet.

My Master's eye was on me, in class. He had judged, that I might respond to poetry. He suggested that four or five of us should read some of a Shakespeare play in his cabin on Sunday afternoons. When the time came, I felt that all that kind of life was over for me, was not to be for me, and I did not go. I was grateful to him for the offer, and for much kindness. He tried to interest me in Architecture. All my new faculties were occupied in trying to learn my new life and adapt myself to it; Architecture was outside the main problem. What was of importance to me, then and later, was an engraving hanging in his cabin. In my memory, it was an etched engraving, showing the ship of Odysseus draw-ing close to the Sirens. Under it were the lines:

"Oh, stay, oh, pride of Greece! Ulysses, stay!
Oh, cease thy course, and listen to our lay!
Blest is the man ordain'd our voice to hear,
The song instructs the soul, and charms the ear.
Approach! thy soul shall into raptures rise!
Approach! and learn new wisdom from the wise.
We know whate'er the kings of mighty name
Achiev'd at Ilion in the field of fame;
Whate'er beneath the sun's bright journey lies.
Oh, stay, and learn new wisdom from the wise."

I read these through whenever I entered the cabin; I learned them by heart; they seemed to me to be so very beautiful, and in some way linked to my present life, which my other favourite poems (the early poems of Milton) were not. I did not ask my master about Ulysses and "Ilion in the field of fame". Somehow, those things seemed now to be forbidden to me, hedged from me by a ship's side. My task was to learn to dress to a deck seam and to pass the tucks of an eye-splice. Even now, the state has not been described.

Then, and for years to come, I felt that every pipe by which things of interest had till then flowed into the empty cistern of my mind, had been "chinsed with scupper plugs well-tommed home".

There were compensations. I was with some extraor-dinary people; "the mariners are a pleasant people", as

Cervantes says; I was in a scene of unbelievable beauty, among ships of unspeakable beauty, with rigging more interesting than anything in the world . . . and yet . . . and yet . . . what did I know of the world, and of my mind, and of what would interest it when I knew?

The ship's Library ought to have been better; the River was a sea library without a peer. It contained each week some of the very best steamers in the world; it was the port of all the crack ships; we had the very flower of the ships trading to the United States, South America, the West Indies, Africa and China. We all learned the funnels and the house-flags of these lines in our first few days on board; then, very swiftly, we learned to know each ship at a glance. In those days, there was much Atlantic racing; we followed the passages of each ship with the passion of boys. We looked for the arrival at her buoy of the famous . . . or the flying . . . wondering whether she would lower the record by yet another hour. Of the three chief North Atlantic lines, we knew each ship, her story, her tonnage, and the yard that built her.

We held with the passion of boys that the Mersey sailing ships were the flower of those still remaining. We were right in our belief; those of the Clyde and the Thames were no better. Some of the very best would sometimes anchor near us, in the splendour of the end of a voyage, all smart for port. Sailors were growing scarce everywhere, yet ships were still brought home looking their best. Sometimes, some fine new ship would stay near us in the stream, under a red flag, while she took on board some explosives. Then, she would get her anchor with a song. We would see her crowd heaving round, while the mate peered over her head-rails to watch the cable growing; then, the tug would take charge and she would dwindle down, bound, most probably, to the port of which we daily talked, the romantic city of "Frisco", where seamen were drugged, slung-shotted and sold at forty dollars a head.

When on my way to the Baths in those early weeks, I always looked out for two ships, the *Skirmisher* and the *Wanderer*. Whither and when was the *Wanderer* going to wander? For "Frisco", men said, in a very few more days. After a week of turbulent weather, the word passed that she had sailed. As we came near the Stage we saw that she was gone; "early that morning" one of the ferrymen said.

She had been the first great ship seen by me; I had thought much of her; now that she had gone, I felt a pang, and also a misgiving, for anyone could see and feel that a gale was coming on, and I had learned already, that new gear is untested, and that new crews were mainly drunk.

Coming back from Liverpool, the weather was worse, and the ferrymen said that they would have to suspend services again. It was possible to be drenched with sprays in the ferry boats; it was easy to be half-drowned with them, going off to the ship in the cutters. We huddled down under the big tarpaulin boat rugs and were glad to get aboard. As soon as the last of us was aboard, the cutters were hoisted, and the launch "hauled out and securely moored" with soul and body lashings fit for the weather.

There was no doubt about the wickedness of the weather; it worsened fast. During the evening, while we were merry-making in our different ways, the C.P.O. came round the main deck with a list in his hand. "There will be anchor watches all through tonight," he said, "it's going to be very bad weather. It's bad for any boat already."

He warned the petty officers on his list what watches they would have to stand. The rule was, for two petty officers to stand an anchor watch together on the upper deck for two hours at a time, keeping a good look-out, with a special eye to the riding lights. They were usually warned, that moorings have been known to part in foul weather. This responsibility, and the fact that you could usually choose your chum, made anchor watches exceedingly popular. There were also side attractions of hot coffee and supper in the galley after the watch. In case of fog, the special watchers had to make "four bells" on the fog bell once (or was it twice?) in every minute; this was less fun.

It was an evil night, followed by a wild morning, with a big sea running, and no communication with the shore. All the gulls had come inland; all the dock walls had a great run of sea along them. Men going down the gangway for a bucket of water had to watch their time.

As the Chaplain could not come off, the Skipper took the services, and preached. This was a new experience to most of us. It brought the Skipper to a position from which he could survey all the worshippers from very close quarters. I had not seen the ship's company so devout; no pins went into any new chum; no ribaldry went into the hymns. All the responses were given with fervour and unction; there were no little gasps of "Ow" or "Stop it" in solemn moments. The effect was very fine, though possibly it was not counted to the crew for righteousness. When the sermon began, we were spell-bound. Our Captain was, at all times, a most excellent, ready public speaker. I have heard many speakers in my day, some of them among the best of the time either as preachers or orators; very few among them have uttered what stayed in the mind ten minutes; and very few indeed have had our Captain's power of being pointed and pithy on any subject at a moment's notice. He was a man of unusual reading, whose mind had searched far and gathered much. He now preached to us upon a sailor's interpretation of a text of St. Paul. Its effect upon the ship's company was profound. There was a general feeling in the congregation that we ought to applaud, though this was stifled by the fact of its being a religious service. I have never heard a better sermon. When we were dismissed, all hands praised it. One young tough, who did very well at sea, said that if

he were C.P.O., instead of a d——d topman whom nobody loved, he would take the thanks of the ship's company straight to the Skipper, and ask for a Liverpool
Leave on the strength of it.

This ought to have been done. I wish that it had been
done, or that, at the least, some senior P.O. had asked
that it might be printed in the ship's paper, but between awe and idleness, the chance was missed.

Later in the week, word came to us that the *Wanderer* had come to some disaster, of dismasting and
death; we knew not exactly what. It was wild autumn
weather for some days.

Then, on the morning of the following Sunday,
there was cold, bright weather, with fog in the lower
River, so much that a fog watch was set, with orders to
strike the bell signal if it thickened in the Sloyne. I was
on deck, somewhere aft, in one of the morning intervals, when there came a great cry of "the *Wanderer*,"
and all hands on deck at the moment rushed to the
focsle head. It was flood tide; we headed down River.
As I reached the top of the focsle head (in those days, a
space easily big enough for thirty or forty men), the
men further forward, at the knightheads cried: "There
she is."

At that instant, the fog in the lower Sloyne went, and
the river there brightened. The *Wanderer* came out
of the greyness into sunlight as a thing of such beauty
as the world can seldom show. She was in the act of pre-
paring to dock with tugs, sidling, so that I saw her

slowly come forward and turn away. She had been
lopped at all her cross-trees, and the wreck of her upper
spars was lashed in her lower rigging. As she turned,
her tattered sails (nearly all were tattered), suddenly
shone all over her; her beautiful sheer, with its painted
ports, shone. I had seen nothing like her in all my life,
and knew, then, that something had happened in a
world not quite ours.

For some time after that, our artists employed
upon setting-in books drew four-masted barques with
painted ports. To myself, the painted port seemed the
only right painting for a ship's hull. I, too, strove to
draw barques with painted ports. Desire outran performance, as is the way in matters of art. How do men
draw such things as the firm, exquisite, sweeping, curv-
ing sheer, with its leaping strakes? Then, having drawn
these miracles, how do they chequer the white space
with oblong, black, painted ports, each exactly the same
size, each the same distance from his fellow, each pre-
cisely edged?

Painters tell me that it is easy. Alas, art is never easy,
and life goes by at speed; you must catch your bird as
it flies. Mind the passing minute; it is all you have.

Once or twice in every term, one or two barbers
came aboard in the forenoon, to cut the ship's company's hair. They stayed on board during most of the
day, working on the port side of the lower deck, amid
a growing heap of clippings. As usual, the seniors were

clipped first (those who wished to be cut), and this had sometimes strange results.

The barbers came on board about a month after I had joined; and began to cut the senior heads. After break that morning, when we returned to our forms, a little focsleman at the end of my row was weeping. I asked my neighbour what the man was weeping for. He said: "Some of the port fore got him, to practise barber on, and they've cut his hair in flights of stairs. They're going to cut all the focsles' the same, they say."

I looked at the weeping lad. His hair had been cut "in flights of stairs"; it was all deeps and marks like a seaman's lead-line, terraced, like cedar boughs; horrible to have to endure, but very funny to see. I must say, I dreaded to be treated thus, and had some qualms about meeting the port fore after school. However, I was spared. We of the Fourth were sent down to be cut during the next two lessons; and the weeping focsleman was trimmed evenly, so that none could tell where the stairs had been.

But the taste for hair had now been stirred in the port fore. Some of them had taken to wearing sheath-knives, sailor fashion, at their backs, under their tunics, the sheaths pointing down their spines. It dawned on these men, that they might be Red Indians and lift the scalps of the pale-faces (the focslemen) since they were thwarted of the joy of barbering. After dinner that day, before we were piped to seamanship, the braves went out on the war-path, and terrible things were done.

They got me down on the boundless prairie somewhere beyond the dreary Black Hills, and though they did not lift my scalp off, and though the barber had left no great harvest for them, they sawed off what there was as close to the roots as they could get. It was excruciatingly painful, but a great stimulus to the hair roots.

Though H.B. had shown me how to avoid being let down at night, I expected to be pitched out again; I turned in nightly, sure of some trial or other before the morning call. Waking in one of those early nights, at some noise not far off, I saw two figures creeping about, now beside hammocks, now dodging under them, pausing over one or two sleepers, and presently violently slapping a face more than usually exposed. As the sleeper woke with a cry, the figures disappeared under hammocks.

This face slapping could seldom be done with effect unless the sleeper used a stretcher at his head clues, to give himself an open space over his pillow. A man tried to do it to me once, soon after this. He did not hit me; he hit the canvas hammock selvage, and wakened me, nothing more. I was not again let down nor pitched out, but the worst of all these night trials was played on me soon afterwards.

I woke up suddenly at midnight, wondering what had happened. I was not sure that I had wakened: indeed, I felt sure that I was caught in a nightmare, unable to wake; I could not open my eyes, and though I rubbed them, they would not open; nor see; they only began to smart. My mouth too, was full of unspeakable sweetish disgustingness, which gave me strong inclination to be sick. I could not waken; I could not know what had happened. With a great effort, I struggled up; forced my eyes open, plucked something from my mouth and looked to see what it was. I had been smeared, eyes and mouth with blacking well moistened and applied liberally with a clout. I cleaned myself up as well as I could with my sponge, and then again turned in. I have supposed since then that I had been snoring; however, a new chum did not have to snore to earn these attentions. I have shrunk from the taste of blacking ever since. Port wine is said to be made from it; when that convivial bowl is offered to me, I guard' 'e pass'.

One November night, I was wakened by a sound of low voices near my hammock. I sat up with a start, expecting enemies, and found two men, standing with the watchman at the port staring at something.

"What is it?" I asked.

"A ship on fire," they said.

I turned out at once, to look with them.

It was a still November night, with a clear sky and a making tide. In one of the Liverpool docks a ship was burning with swiftly growing fury; the light was cast as it were in splashes, as from buckets, on warehouses and the near-by ships. It was beautiful as thing could be, and then suddenly became superb. Long afterwards, in the tropics, I saw a forest fire run down the side of a mountain with a speed which taught me what is meant by the phrase "like wild fire". As we watched, the fire in this burning ship suddenly became its living lord. Perhaps the fire was amidships, somewhere, very likely in or near her main hatch. Now, like a smart hand leaping into the rigging, it hopped beyond the sheer pole, and up the shrouds. Instantly, almost as though fire had been hoisted like flags, in made up balls to be twitched open as they reached their place, the masts, yards and rigging were all licked and bright with pennons of fire. This was unspeakably lovely for a few seconds; and then, when we were sure that the splendour would become tenfold, it darkened suddenly.

"Too much smoke, now," the watchman explained to us, "the firemen are getting her under control. Turn in, now, before you all catch cold."

One other hammock memory remains. Once in every term, we drew clean hammocks, and sent the old ones to be washed and restencilled. We removed the clues and nettles from our old hammocks and affixed them to the clean canvas. It was this process which utterly puzzled the new chum. It sounds so easy. All you have to do is to hitch sixteen nettles to the eyes in the canvas at each end, and there your bed is, ready. It looked so easy. But, oh, when I was once in the throes of it, all was tangled and despairing. Red Swab looked at my effort, and said: "Stop. You've got a thorough-foot."

With a couple of adroit dips and twiddles, he made all clear for me: I went on again into even greater con-

fusion, till Dick came by and said: "Stop. You've got a
through-fit."

With a few more twiddles he made all clear for me.
I went on again into a kind of chaos. Very nearly all
the two focsles were like me, puzzled, confused and
helpless. I am sorry to have to say that it took us most
of the afternoon to shift hammocks. One of the old
naval Instructors looked at us with wonder, and said:
"Do you know how long we're allowed for shifting
hammocks in the Navy? Two minutes."

The old hands drifted down to gaze and sniff. The
silent gaze, the pitying sniff, is there any criticism bit-
terer? I dreaded the next shifting hammocks more than
I can say; but when the time came, I found that I could
do it. We never beat the Navy, of course; who can?

At every sweeping of the deck, I came upon trial
pieces flung away by seamen, mostly bits of spun-yarn,
with splices or strand knots worked (or begun) upon
them, scraps of marline in process of becoming mats,
or pieces of canvas partly seamed. Like everyone on
board, I came to love having spun-yarn about me. I
loved the smell, and the ease with which it worked.
Slowly, knot by knot and strand by strand, I came to
know the knots and splices; and with my pocket piece
could practise them in school, when the lesson seemed
dull. I always carried spun-yarn; and when I found any
interesting splice or knot in the litter of the deck I got
a man to tell me what it was and how to make it.

Slowly, from watching the shipping, I came to understand the process of tacking ship; and, more slowly, the points which make the beauty of a ship; and, more slowly still, how to judge her tonnage.

In nearly all sailing ships of that time, the lines forward were of an exciting grace. Often, the curve of the hull, the sweep of the sheer, from forward aft, was of an agreeable bird-like balance. Sometimes, especially in the newer ships, the builders escaped from all suggestion of the old wooden stern constructions, transom or rounded, and made something fitter to the new material, finishing the counters with the most delicate, merging ellipses.

Above this horizontal fabric of such varying charm rose the raking, tapering pinnacles of three or four masts, each subtly diminishing in size and raiment, each proud, efficient, and a beauty adding to beauty.

All sailing ships had some measure of these graces: some had them surpassingly. To those with an eye for a ship, a feeling for what makes a ship, these were things of sublime and tragic beauty. As in the ballet, the young queen was the exquisite adored one. On that fierce stage of the sea, in that grim day, the hope of many an owner soon showed a working loss.

Illusion is an artist's world: by charming sounds, pure lines, and the noble colours he makes an illusion, which may be truth, and will surely make truth easier to bear.

Somewhere in offices and mould lofts, little known

men were creating these ships daily, for the roughest service of men, yet giving to each some quality which made her as a living queen to all who saw and served.

Some (not very old) men aboard us said that we boys were born too late, that we could not know nor imagine what ships could be. To them the glory of the ship had been in 1854-5, when our fleets sailed for the Crimea and the Baltic. There are prints of those sailings; indeed, few pageants can have been grander. Others of our elders said: "It is not so; the great day of the sailing ship was later, by ten years, in the time of the clipper ship, the Australian voyage and the Tea Race from the Min River. The clippers were the ships," these men said, "their crews were the sailors".

There are prints of these ships, too: something exquisite was there. Each decade has a splendour of its own, which only the young can know: ours, too, had a glory: but few prints were being made of ours. The best of any time is good: we had the best of ours.

I was beyond all mortals lucky in seeing and knowing something of those decades of the sailing ship, the three in which she touched perfection, as man-of-war, as bird of passage, and as carrier. I was in one of the men-of-war; I saw some of the birds, all broken-winged, poor souls; the carriers filled the docks.

Thinking of ships fills the mind with images of power, elegance and grace. A harbour is something of a dancing place set for a performance: the sea-port makes the décor: the ships, the figures of the dancers, moving to the roar of toil, the hooting of sound signals, and the cries and songs of men.

A ship must have manly power, to survive. Her designers gave her that. Almost always, in giving her that with their whole hearts, they added something which keeps their work alive in memory half a century after the sea took it.

Though H.B. had gone, I remembered all he had told me, especially, how necessary it was for me to get to know modern rigging practise.

We knew very well, that we were living in an age of revolution in all sea affairs. We knew (at least, all our lively ones knew), that the sailing ship would soon vanish. For the moment, she was being fitted to serve the few trade routes over which she could compete with steamers (the West Coast, Australia). She was being built big, with a plentiful use of iron in her masts and of chain and wire in her rigging; and with many devices, such as double yards, donkey engines, Hadfield deck capstans, brace winches, spike bowsprits, etc., to make her cheap to run.

Our rig and routine, were naval, dating from 1865-70; the men who taught us had been shipmates with the old gear and stood for the old routine; they almost all thought that it was *vital* to us to know the numbers of the inner and outer turns of the reef ear-rings! it was a stock question in exams. Almost all of them thought that it was important that we should know how to sling a (naval) top. This was an ingenious process, I grant,

but of what use then, even in the Navy? I found myself
in a young community almost wholly against our teaching. We knew what ships had been in 1865-70; lots of
them, with fossils of the old rigs still on them, passed
in the river each week, all bound for Dead Man's Bay.
What we approved, was the ship of our own time, the
big four-master, the thing we called a four-masted
barque, and Americans a four-masted ship. (Let us not
quarrel over it; both sides are right; the barque has
no yards on her aftermost mast; the ship has yards on
her mizen mast.)

With a borrowed glass aloft, I could see lots of those
big four-masters in dock and longed to be aloft in them,
doing H.B.'s bidding, and learning the modern practise.

As I have said, we preferred lofty ships, with masts,
that went up, and rose, and over-topped, and out-
towered. These were more frequent among Scottish
and American fleets than in English; and more remark-
able in the American ships than in the Scottish. In those
days, the American forests yielded superb spars which
no other forests could grow; and certainly the American sea instinct was to give their ships every power and
grace that could be given. When the word passed that
a wonder of a ship had docked, our excitement was
intense; we gazed and gazed.

Remember, reader, that these ships docked in superb
sea order, newly painted, freshly tarred down, with
colours flying, every yard squared by the lifts and

braces, and very often every yard mast headed, with the sails in exquisite harbour stows, and white as so much American canvas is. Once, too, there was a marvel, a wonder entered, and lay there for a few days. She had three skysails and a main moonsail. We watched her with leaping hearts, marvelling, and hoping that she would still be there when we could get to her; we all meant to reach that moonsail yard, so that we could say: "When the . . . was in dock we laid out on her moonsail yard." Alas, her stay was brief; we never even learned what she was; and no other moonsail yarder ever swam into our ken.

Suddenly, there was an irruption of seniors into the focsles. Some of the toughest and most exclusive seniors were among us, talking as if they really rather liked us, and offering us all sorts of things at bargain prices: books, knives, purses, sail-makers' tools, instruments, rulers, parts of kit, trousers, shoes, etc., and things which had been birthday or Christmas presents. A man said to me: "Don't you buy anything. Keep your money. They've heard that the C.P.O. is going to ask for a Liverpool Leave tonight and they're raising the wind for going ashore tomorrow."

This was good advice, based on knowledge of the ship, and I should have been wise to hearken. There came to me, as I sat on my chest under the port, a certain tough senior of the port mizen, a fellow with an odd name and a reckless way. He had a book for sale, a red book, a present if I remember rightly, from his loving aunt the Christmas before. It was a copy of *Treasure Island,* with the old illustrations ("the artist has got his types up in Hogarth," Stevenson said). This was now offered at a bargain price. I bought it; the map alone was worth the money I gave for it.

Stevenson was alive then, at the other side of the world. I wish that I had written to tell him what ecstasy that book gave me. I started to read it there and then, with the feeling that it had been written for me, and that no boy in the wide world could be enjoying it as I did. All the characters were on board with me. Long John Silver, though with two legs and without any parrot, was in the port fore. Billy Bones and old Pew were in the port main. Merry was in the fourth class with me. All our officers were touched off to the life; Squire, Doctor and Alexander Smollett; we had a Benn Gunn in the starboard main; and out of two ruffians, senior and sinister, one could have made a Flint. I had bought and paid for this treasure; it was probably the first book I bought for myself; and I was deep in its wonder, when an old battered tarpaulin of the port watch, who would have served for Israel Hands, asked me if I would buy a chest lashing. (They used to call them "chest-lashers" in those days.) The lasher then was a length of line or cord about sixteen feet long, with an eye-slice at one end, and sometimes a point worked on the other. It was used to secure one's chest when going home for the holidays; we all used them; the official price was a shilling. As the man said: "You'll have to have one, for going home," but this man sold me his for sixpence. He was a man who had a great deal of respect from us, because he had let it be known, that no matter what good things he might do in the years remaining to him, he was certain to go to hell after death; he was damned, he said. He would not tell us what he had done, though many asked, from desire to share his distinction. "I shall be in hell forever," he said, "whatever I do, I am damned."

I met him in a far-off sea-port forty years later; he had done very well in this life; and I did not ask him how he felt about the next. He seemed to be bearing up pretty well.

Still, on this autumn evening, he sold me his chest lasher for sixpence, present pay; and those who witnessed the deal said that I was a —— young ass to chuck my money away, first on a book and then on a something chest lasher, when any something fool could tell that there would be a Liverpool Leave tomorrow. Life in the ship was public; every personal deal was witnessed, commented upon and criticised. I had made, as it happened, two good bargains, and by some fortunate windfall had still tester in pouch for the morrow. I went on with my reading of *Treasure Island,* marvelling more and more at Stevenson's knowledge of marine character. The illustrations puzzled me slightly; the *Hispaniola* was described as a schooner, yet this artist showed her with yards on her mainmast. Schooners, usually topsail schooners, were daily in the river,

the rig was intimately familiar to all of us. As it was a
free evening, I read on and on; and at eight bells, as I
had not to sweep, I took the book to one of the Instructors, to ask him about the yards. I was a little shy of
some of the Instructors still, but this one was one of
the best of them. I found him outside the Instructors'
berth on the main deck, talking with a second Instructor about the difference between a plantain and a yam,
and how it could always be told by a midship section.
When the other had gone, I asked this old seaman, if
he could explain this matter of the yards. He looked at
the illustrations, and said: "There used to be that kind
of schooner. She was called a 'two-topsail schooner' or
a 'maintopsail schooner'. When the Runcorn Fleet goes
out, you may see one still, for very likely there will
be one. They're getting rare, now." I was delighted to
have this knowledge, and promptly used it to quench
a critic who had condemned the artist for ignorance.
Half a century later, I learned that Stevenson thought
that the artist had made his schooner a brig. Stevenson
himself adds to our puzzle by talking of "mizzen
shrouds", (Chapter XXVI).

The talk now ran upon a holiday the next day, if it
were but reasonably fine. Being new chums, we did not
know Liverpool, and rather shrank from going alone.
Following the custom of the ship, we began to choose
our companions for the day. I was friendly with almost
all my focsle; three of us held a muster of money, and
decided to pool it. Word went about that the weekly

pocket-money would be paid before we went ashore; and with what we already had, we were not badly off. We planned the day with care.

Red Swab told us, that we should be expected to go to the Walker Art Gallery, to see the Autumn Exhibition; the ship's company was always invited to this, and everybody went to it, because there were always paintings of ships, jolly well worth seeing. We should enjoy it, he said, and, besides, sometimes the Masters made us write an account of it next day; "still, they were only pictures, we need not stay long." Then, there were the Baths, the Cornwallis Street Baths, the docks, and the *Eagle,* for the main delights of the day, and a great variety of tuck shops for the support of fainting nature. We agreed, that the first thing to do would be the Art Gallery, "to get it over"; after that, we could go to the Cornwallis Street Baths, and stay in to the very limit of human endurance; then lunch in some sort of a tuck shop; then go along the docks and aboard the *Eagle;* then go to the Baths, "and never mind if the seniors do cut up rough; they can't kill us," then tuck of some sort at Simpsons, and so back aboard by the last possible ferry.

I am told, that the Liverpool Leave is no longer a delight of the ship's company. It was decided many years ago that Liverpool was not the sort of place for growing boys, and this, although the city had changed much for the better since the time of which I write. In my day, a Liverpool Leave left memories of joy forever;

and if, in my time, six men played the fool there, they would have been no wiser elsewhere.

The morrow dawned fair. We hurried through the morning work; and as we cleaned our deck were visited by men of the working top, who came to bribe the bigger men of our focsle to take their places in the day's cutter. I was a little fellow, and had no offer, but big sums were there for any who wished to sell his freedom. At Hands. Dress, we smartened up for shore, so as to be ready in case, and so went up to Prayers.

After Prayers, we all turned to the Skipper; we were all on tenter hooks, and the Skipper's face gave no sign of any sort. He took the Gunner's report; and then turned to us with a smile. "As it is such a fine day, I think we had better get that Liverpool Leave out of the way." When the Skipper was terrible, he was terrifying; but when he meant to be nice no man could be more winning. We knew being boys, fairly shrewdly, that he was glad of our enthusiasm but liked it to be ordered. Instantly, the C.P.O. called for three cheers for him; and after these had been given, we dashed below for uniform caps, and a last little polish to our boots. At once, there came the pipe for Liberty Men to fall in; we, who were Liberty Men, fell in, and were soon wafted away, running the marvellous River in a ferry. That, in itself, was joy enough; but we had before us, the prospect of all day free, with pictures, Baths, ships and tuck to fleet the time pleasantly till the late ferry. Some of the tougher men tried to borrow money from us; we were not quite such asses; we knew those men a little by this time; besides, this was our first Liverpool Leave, and our money was no longer our own; it belonged to the syndicate.

On landing at the Stage, my party set out for the Art Gallery. In those days, the George's Dock lay between the Stage and the city, and traffic was sometimes held up while a ship towed past. We stopped at the side of the George's Dock to look at the ships there. Though we had been on board only a few weeks, we had learned already to look at ships almost as if they were living things. Those in the George's Dock were all small vessels waiting to be sold; one or two of them had straw brooms lashed to their mastheads, to show this. I remember three of them to this day, a small, old coasting steamer, very dirty; a neat, fine, steam yacht, very dainty, with a lot of unnecessary brasswork on her deck and in the treads of her ladders, and a small West Coast barque. We rejected the coaster; we went aboard the yacht, made eight bells upon her bell, judged that her gear would be just the right size for us to handle, and admired her gimcrack finish. She was only a toy, but we were in the toy ship stage.

After this, we went aboard the barque, and asked her caretaker, if we might go over her. He showed her to us. She was a little, old thing, just over seven hundred tons. She had a look of having come down in the world, but was not yet uncared-for. I asked if we might see the half deck, where the apprentices berthed. The man thrust open a scuttle on the booby hatch, abaft the mainmast, and going down some steep iron stairs I found myself in a sort of morgue eight feet square with stretchers for four corpses. I was shocked at the smallness and the darkness. I knew already, that in big seas that part of a modern ship was often under water; and I could not understand what kept the boys there from being drowned or suffocated. If the scuttle were open, the berth would fill to the brim; if the scuttle were shut neither light nor air could enter. I asked the caretaker about this. He said: "They did all right." Her sails were unbent; the running rigging was all unrove; we looked at her gear, and decided that she was a rather potty little old thing, not worth going aloft in. There was nothing much to learn from her, and after our own spars, these seemed like toothpicks. We were all for big ships, and despised these follies of our fathers. Yet she was the first ocean-going sailing vessel I had ever been aboard; and I remember her to this day. After we left her, I took a good look at her. She was not much for looks; she had a somewhat loutish stern, and aloft, the usual minimum. Long afterwards, I met a man who had been in her. He said that she could go when driven, but that her great merit was her dryness; she kept her decks dry, and that the half deck was "as dry as a bone". When I spoke with him, I had learned how romantic a ship may come to seem in memory. I doubted that dryness; all the same, there he was undrowned, a living proof. I know not what became of her. I suppose that some foreigner bought her cheap, renamed her and ran her till she came to grief or ceased to pay. As those little old iron ships were very strongly built, she may exist as a coal hulk somewhere, little as she was. I have a memory for ships, and have cast many a searching look upon many an old coal hulk; so far I have not seen her. Of her bones, I judge, is coral made, if she hasn't been salved to make bombs.

Now that we had sampled the George's Dock, we followed groups of our shipmates up the hill towards the Gallery. Soon, I was looking at the first exhibition of modern painting I had ever seen. Red Swab was right; there were some paintings of ships, "jolly well worth seeing", including one of a big ship of the old sailing Navy becalmed at sunset, with a rosy glow upon her sails. This was the work which took our fancy. This was something which no man of our painters had yet attempted, the wrinklings running in unfilled canvas, and the colour of Nature. All the ship's painters gathered before this work, and wondered how he did it, and whether it was a dodge which could be learned. We looked at our chief painter; like us, he was laid low by a greater skill than his. He was a confident fellow, he soon recovered his poise. Give him a little time, he seemed to say, and his natural talent would do things as fair. It was not so with me. I had begun to try to draw, and having no talent whatever that way, found only endless delight and never-failing disappointment. It is true, that once, as I drew at a desk on the main deck, one clumsy mariner said of me: "This chum isn't a bad drorer" (that was the word he used). One, prompted by this word to look at my droring (perhaps that is the word to describe it) said rather cuttingly: "She's the ship that never returned, isn't she?" Now I looked at this painting bigger than myself with an ecstasy of pleasure mixed with an anguish of despair. Oh, to be able to do that, and to do it all my life, squeezing lovely colours out of tubes, and setting down the exquisite, fair ships who lay within sight of me, in all their beauty, in all their tragedy. One thing I could do. I could, perhaps, get some oil colours and try this marvel for myself. Kind old Mr. Kiddie would be aboard on Friday; I could ask him about it. I found the Art Gallery such a place of enchantment that I was not eager to leave it, till my friends pointed out, that paintings were all very well but by no means the only joy. Out we went, exploring, and picking up the simple plan of the city. The Waxworks tempted us a little; the Market tempted rather more. We had been told not to miss a certain shop in a very fishy quarter; we did not miss it; then, having sated our eyes with its delights, we found a tuck shop of which we had heard great things. Here we feasted on the common fund, and then set forth for the docks.

Ships were small, then, and being, small, many were needed. We, as future sailors, and as it were, the children of that great sea-port, were privileged beings though we did not know it. We were allowed to go

almost anywhere among the docks which were almost
always full of ships of kinds no longer seen, each one
touched with a power, if not with a beauty, each one
rigged by a different master rigger, and some of them
superb, one or two of them supreme. From my first
going aloft, rigging had become an absorbing interest
to me. H.B. had urged me to learn the modern practise;
now I had the chance to see it, to handle it, and tread its
dreadful stairs. You may remember with what rapture
you, in your boyhoods, went to the circus. I was going
to the docks, to see ships, possibly a hundred ships,
some of them the latest and most splendid. Our knowledge of ships was about six weeks old; few would have
guessed this from our talk. On our way, we saw a sight,
new to us then, which later became familiar. A big
ship's crowd was on its way to be paid off. They had
been in her, by their look, a year or more, and had a
good pay-day coming to them. They had the indescribable look of high endurance, which used to mark the
sailing-ship seaman. During and just after the last war
one saw the same look on the faces of some of the infan-
try. I have seen it on no other faces. With these men,
whose manhood had brought perhaps three thousand
tons of cargo half round the world, were the harpies
who meant to drug and rob them. These creatures,
male and female, hung upon them. Pew would have
been a gentleman beside some of those blowflies. I was
a little boy, but the plan of these villains was so clear
that I could not mistake it. One of my companions, who

knew a little of seaport life, said: "They won't have their wages long." I saw so clearly, what was happening. These men were like children, from being so long away from the land. They had known only manhood and shipmates; now they were ashore among scum and sneak-thieves. Nobody seemed to mind. These men had kept and defended and brought home some merchant's ship, at the risk of their lives; now, they were going to be robbed of their earnings. It was clear to all that they were going to be robbed; it did not seem to matter. People had seen the same thing almost daily. They smiled at the sight, fine fellows, who were going to be fools; clever fellows, who were going to be rich without working. The crew passed by, with those maggots of corruption clinging to them. (They had the faces and the minds of maggots.) Several times in my childhood I had been appalled by the callousness of life: I was appalled, then; it was a scene most frightful to me. Well, later, I was to see other instances of men who did the work at the risk, or cost, of their lives, for the benefit of harpies. The game goes on still.

We crossed the great road on which the giant grey dray-horses dragged the cotton lorries, with a crash of calkins smiting fire. That was one of the sights of the port, then, most noble. It went on all day, team after team, dragging piled bales from which the tufts of cotton thrust. All day, the shags of the hoofs stamped the blocks of the road, with a clash, a clink, and a spurt of sparks. The lorry men swore or cheered; the whips cracked, the leather grunted and chain clanked. I was always in a kind of dream when I saw these things. I knew that all the cotton had grown in the sun many thousands of miles away, that negroes had hoed it and picked and baled it; that it had been swung aboard and clattered down into a hold, by men at winches, whips and capstans; that then it had been steeved into a jam, with perhaps strange creatures of the South, snakes, birds, animals, butterflies, for I knew that all these were sometimes found, and so brought in a whining whick-ering sea passage to this port of mine. It was almost more than I could endure sometimes, to think that all this world of man's toil and triumph was mine; there it was, visibly mine; all that clatter, all those masts, all that pageant of the River at flood. Now, I was going into the docks; not the George's Docks, of the dead ships; but the real docks, where the ships that H.B. bade me learn were lying; fifty of them; perhaps a hundred.

We met with another party of men going to the docks, and followed them, partly because we did not know our way about, and partly because we doubted that we were free to go where we chose. We came into a great warehouse and an overwhelming reek of or-anges. A tramp was discharging oranges; crates of oranges were heaped there; slings, with more crates were running up, swaying and collapsing down. Corpses of oranges floated in the dock, trodden oranges lay on the warehouse floor; one or two crates had come to grief, it seemed. There were many stevedores about; there were piles of merchandise waiting to be shipped; all sorts of sea smells, low water; tar, paint, turpentine, creosote, engine-room, came to us from the enormous travelling doors. We came out into a dock where sailing ships lay alongside, in every stage of discharge. I saw for the first time, the timber ships, with the holes cut in their bows for the discharge of the logs. I had heard of this, and had not believed; now I saw it in practise. There were the ships from the great cutting in Oregon, and as I watched, the runners travelled and logs thrust out, jerked forward, and went into the water. Near these, was a wooden Norwegian barque, with a windmill set and revolving. I had often seen these in the river, not far away; and had been told that the windmill was the Norwegian house-flag. It was, of course, a pump clearing the bilges; and seeing it working, I wished that we had one to lessen our morning toil; but judged that we stood too high out of the water.

Most of the ships had been smartened up for port, and had not lost all their brightness. I was attracted by the decorations. I wanted to look at figureheads and the gay paintings of house-flags on scuttle butts and boats. The friend who knew a little of sea life, said that I could find all the colours I wanted in canal barges. I was newer to ships than he; I was not yet sated with these delights. Figureheads thrusting up above me from tail boards, bow fasts, and coils of gear, were things I had often read of; now here they were, Queens, Nymphs, ladies with spears, bows, torches; then Indian princes, Moors of Venice, Kings, Nelsons. Ships were still being built with figureheads; to me, they seemed from the first an essential to a ship's appearance. My friend said: "Oh, come on. I want to see some clippers. Nobody wants figureheads in these days; they use scroll-work or fiddleheads now. You can see a figurehead all day long in our —— old Noah's Ark in the River there."

This was not strictly true. To get a good look at our figurehead one had to clamber down a difficult way, with the certainty of rousing the Officer of the Watch to a suspicion that you were going there to smoke; a suspicion often just. However, I supposed then, that there would be figureheads all through my life; there would be time later on for figureheads. (I had time to see a good many.) We went on, till, suddenly, there just ahead, was the *Eagle,* with Dick at her gangway. Dick hailed us and told us to come aboard. We went up, feeling ourselves in luck. She was (I believe), a French prize, built in the eighteenth century, and now converted into a Drill Ship. Below, she seemed like a ship of another world; above, she was boxed over with a roomy superstructure, in which sea cannon were mounted. Naval reservists lived on board while doing their drills; and drills were in progress as we entered. Dick had a relative on board, a Lieutenant, who welcomed us all, and showed us the ship.

I was often aboard her later; but I cannot forget the thrill of that first time. The modern Navy was divided into guns' crews about us. A Lieutenant, taking the drill, was directing the guns upon parts of the ships near-by. He was calling: "Port Battery, upon the bow; Starboard Battery, upon the beam. Carry on." Then some numbers hove upon wheels, and other numbers hauled upon side tackles; and the cannon swung on to their targets. Our host told us to come on down; he showed us a hatch; and in an instant, I was away from the modern Navy aboard the *Hispaniola,* going below into the eighteenth century. The hatchway rail was coach whipped with new white line, a miracle of plaiting; then, there we were on what had once been her main deck; and strange as the main deck was, it was commonplace to her lower deck. Captain Flint might have died on the lower deck; it belonged to men with pigtails, who drank rum from pannikins. It was so low and so dark that it made us all stoop instinctively. It was the deck Israel Hands had been gunner on, and at one or other of those ports, old Pew had lost his dead lights. To myself, all fresh from *Treasure Island,* the sight of that old ship was an entrancement of romance. I could have stayed there all day.

The *Eagle* was there for many years, before being broken up. When destroyed, she must have been almost the oldest ship in the world. Alas, I am told, that she was allowed to go unrecorded. Perhaps no drawing, no photograph, no measurement remains of those strange romantic decks in their exquisite order. Well . . . I saw them, at the time I was best fitted to enjoy them. I came out of the ship, to the dock-side in a dream of ecstasy. I said something polite to the kind officer who had taken us round; in my thought, I believe that I have thanked him daily ever since. Who could have thought, from the black band-box-fabric outside, that the ship held such wonders within? I said something to my companions about what I supposed to be the newness and the power of the cannon on her drill deck. The more knowing of my mates sniffed, and said: "What? Those poor old things?" and sniffed again. Feeling somewhat crushed, I said that it was jolly decent of Dick to have given us the chance of going with him. This he agreed to; Dick was a jolly good chap. What happened to Dick? He went to sea, and did well; he was a born sailor. He was soon second mate in a crack ship. On a dark night off the Horn a big sea took him overboard. He was "all lashed up" in sea boots and oilskins, the oilskin trousers stopped with ropeyarn over the boots. The weight of water in these things must soon have taken him down, even if the weight of the sea did not sweep him down forever as it took him. I have a letter from his Mother, telling me of these things.

We had not far to go to find a clipper worth boarding. There was a big, new four-master of over two thousand five hundred tons, with her hatches not yet off, and her paint all smart for coming home. Though her sails had been unbent, her running rigging was aloft still. We went up her gangplank, and found her mate on deck, smoking a pipe on a coaming. Very respectfully, we advanced to him in the regulation manner, halted, took off our caps, advanced one step, and waited to be spoken to. He smiled somewhat grimly at this performance, and said: "Well, boys, what is it?"

"Please, sir, may we go over the ship, and up aloft?"

"Go anywhere you like."

"Thank you, sir."

She was the first big modern ship I had been aboard. I must say, that my first impression of her was overwhelming. The mate suddenly called us back, with:

"Boys."

"Sir."

"Don't put your feet through the garboard strakes."

We did not in the least know what he meant; we knew an order when we heard it.

"Very good, sir," we said.

We scattered further forward to sort our impressions, and decided that garboard strakes were probably something flimsy in the awning or skylight way. They might be light gratings somewhere; it would never do to show that we did not know. As long as we watched our steps and went delicately it would be all right. We took a look aloft, and let our eyes travel down the shrouds. We were used to the outboard chains, with deadeyes, of the ancient rig. Now we saw the inboard screws of our own time. We were used to the skinny bitts and fiferails serving two sails to a mast. Now we saw the full fairleads, heaped pins, pendants and falls controlling six big square sails and four staysails at each mast. The gear was endless, and all new and all good, much choice hemp, much exquisite new manilla, and a lot of chain, where strains had become too much for rope. It was clear to us all that this was something like a ship; even our companion who knew more than we two, admitted that she was a —— fine ship; and had the grace to say that he couldn't think what all the gear was for. It was that same point which puzzled us. The size of the braces and the power of the crab stopper, which we handled, and gingerly squeezed our hands with, gave us all a sense that this kind of ship was facing force with strength; there was nothing of the toy in this creature. I went up the iron ladder to the top of the midship house. All the doors of the houses were locked, because ship thieves and dock rats had a fondness for what could be found. I could look down the skylight into the bare iron tanks in which men lived. The top of the deck-house was heaped with coiled staysail sheet gear. A boat lay on skids on each side of the skylight. As my friends had started aloft, I left my house top, and went up the starboard main rigging.

When the ship had met her tug a few days before, she had been upon the port tack, close hauled. She had backed her mainyards for the parley and the passing of the line, and had not touched her braces since. My two friends had started aloft on the port side, and had come to the mainyard almost on the shrouds. It was something new to their experience; they had stopped to admire. I went up on the clear side. I was thrilled by the ship's perfection. The shrouds were new, or almost new; the ratlines were better and newer than ours. As I neared the futtocks, I found the shrouds converging, so that the treads of each ratline were tiny. I was aghast at the chasm between the shrouds and the yard at this point, and at the appalling size of the yard. My main point, was to be in the top before my friends. This I managed. Being in the top I found it floored with a grating, much too strong to put a foot through, and much too small for the top smoking parties which I had seen aboard the lugger. Up above me were the topsail yards, and a multitude of gear leading into blocks and disappearing down. I could not guess what one third of them could be meant for. The spreaders, the catch ratlines and the mighty array of backstays were marvels to me. Certainly H.B. was right; this was what I had to learn. The bigness, the newness and the multitude were terrifying, as he had said they would be; luckily, three of the four masts seemed exactly the same size, with interchangeable gear; even so, there would be the jigger mast, with gear entirely unknown to me.

My favourite perch had been the topmast cross-trees. There they lay high above me, up a pretty steep pair of stairs. Up I went, still finding the gear choicely good and a pleasure to go upon. When I reached the cross-trees, I was higher than I had ever been. The deck was like a pale cigar below me; I had a view of the ships in dock and the River beyond. Up above me was a perch hitherto unknown to me; the topgallant cross-trees, with a royal yard above that, about as big (it seemed), as our mizen topsail yard. As the royal was the boy's portion at sea, I had to see what it was going to amount to; so up I went again.

Like many big ships of the time, she had royal and topgallant masts in one. The topgallant cross-trees seemed a long, long way from home; and again, the royal yard seemed braced far from me. Very gingerly, and with a good deal of fear, for I was now very high up in a world entirely new to me, I got a good hold of something, and stepped on to the footrope. When I was on it, I could lean over the yard and hold on with both hands. This was not enough, however; I had to lay out, to find out if I could do it.

As I had rightly judged, this royal yard was about the size of our mizen topsail yard. It was all right, to edge out a little, but this brought me clear of the mast, over the other yards and the deck; and edging a little further, I came to one of the stirrups, which supported the footrope on which I stood. The footrope moved through the stirrup eye as my weight shifted, and though I was used to this, I was not used to it at that height. I reached the yardarm. I had some scheme of jockeying the yardarm like a reef-ear-ring-man on a topsail. When I reached the yardarm, however, I reflected, that this might not be wise in my best uniform; at least, I may have reflected so; anyhow, I laid in again, and for the act of getting off the footrope, laid hold of something, first with one hand then with the other, and swung myself off to safety. Unfortunately, one of the ropes I held had slack on it; under my weight, it gave, and down I came. I came down about a foot. I was glad at the time that it was no more.

After this, I felt that we ought not to abuse the mate's kindness too long, in letting us go aloft. I came down into the top, and after marvelling a little at the size and strength of the lower topsail yard and its truss, I went down the futtocks to examine the still more impressive main yard, with its great chain topsail sheets. I was glad to find that no one had noticed my little slip aloft.

As H.B. had told me, I felt very queer in the leg, as though I had been riding a cart-horse, when I stood again upon the deck. My friends agreed, that this was certainly a very splendid ship. We went further forward, up the steep rise in her fore deck, to her focsle head, where we compared her capstan and windlass with what we knew. Then eager to learn, we crawled along the spike bowsprit, and had an impressive lesson in the importance of a foremast and the need of making it secure. When we came in again, we looked aft at her sweep. We all felt, and all said, that this was what we should have to learn; why were we wasting time upon the obsolete? Echo answered: Why? We went aft, to the break of the poop, hoping to thank the mate for his kindness; he was no longer there. We did not dare to trespass on to the poop; we took another look round and gaze upwards; then went down her gangway to the dockside.

She had two little Hadfields near her mizen mast. My knowing companion said that these little capstans were wonders; you could lead the topsail-halliards to them or get any spar or weight up by them. I was glad to know that these, too, were things of power; they seemed the only small things there, except ourselves. We talked a little about the garboard strakes. I was not at all sure that the phrase did not mean just the air, and that the mate had meant, "don't come down through the air". I had come pretty near to putting myself through the air for a hundred and fifty feet, or so; Humpty-Dumpty would have been tidy compared with me. However, now came the real delight, the Baths.

We had expected to find them full; they were almost deserted. We could go in at the deep end; we could use the senior dressing-rooms close to the springboards; we had all that heaven on earth pretty much to ourselves. A few men came in while we were there; nearly all of them juniors; the seniors, of course, had gone to bathe elsewhere. As usual, we stayed in the water till we were quaking with cold and our teeth chattering; even so, we hated to come out; if there were other joys in life, they paled beside the ecstasy of the deep-green water ever spouting salt from the mouths in the marble sides. Still quaking, and with shuddering limbs we ran to the Stage and Simpsons. A senior P.O., a very fine fellow, who had been in the water with us, condescended to come with us. He asked what ships we had been aboard. We mentioned our four-master, with praise. He said:

"She is a fine, big ship. I can't say I like her bow." This splendid being let us stand him some tuck, and then, in his turn treated us. This was quite extraordinarily nice of him; our hearts warmed to him. He was one of the cleverest men on board, now that H.B. had gone; and here he was treating new chums out of niceness of heart.

In the ferry, of course, we sorted up with our fellow focslemen. We were sorry to have our leave at an end; I had enjoyed my day more than I could tell. I saw my big ship from the river; there was her main royal yard. The men near me said that she was quite a fine big ship, of course, but too much of the general pattern to please them. They liked something out of the way. The seniors were talking of an American ship, which was utterly out of the way; a three skysail yarder, which always set passaree Angels' Whispers above the skysails. *She* was the ship for their money. They had been up to her trucks, some of them, and thought foul scorn of an English four-master, with nothing above the royals, and "everything standardized". All the way home, we heard of the ships in dock, and of the feats of our seniors; how they had smoked; how some of them had had a port in a pub; and how . . . But a senior from the port watch got hold of me, and said: "You've not passed for a pirate yet?"

I was so plainly puzzled that he explained. "This chum hasn't passed for a pirate yet. He must. What do you say, you chaps?"

"Of course he must," they said. They knew no more

217

than I what was meant, but saw that some devilry was up, and that it would keep one of these new chums from being too —— uppish.

"See here," my senior said, "chums here have to pass for pirate or jolly well jump overboard. You see the man at the wheel there, steering?"

I did. I had often noticed him. He was a melancholy-looking man, who handled the ferry boats with a skill which was a never-failing joy to me.

'You've got to go up to him," my senior said. "You'll say to him with the *Conway's* compliments: '*Skipper Gooseneck, you're not fit to carry guts to a bear: let alone steer a Mersey ferry*'."

As I was not in this man's watch, it is likely that he had not noticed me before and mistook me for an October Boy, much younger and greener than I was. It is true, that I was still a very young and very green hand, but not quite so green as all that. I had enough poetical sense, to know that if anything complimentary had been meant, the term would have been "Swan-neck". I knew that a gooseneck was the tough iron swing pin on a boom end, or, indeed, any forlorn-looking iron bar, such as this helmsman's neck was. Then, there was a notice: *Do not speak to the man at the wheel*. The man's face was another forbidding notice; and my natural courtesy was against any message of the kind. I said I would not do any such thing; and although half a dozen of them urged me on, and said I had to, I refused, and the matter dropped; they moved away.

Yet, within two minutes, they persuaded an unhappy new chum to go at least so far as to call the helmsman "Skipper Gooseneck", not once, but several times. It seemed to me beyond possibility that any new chum could be such an ass. Thrice the brinded kitten mewed; then lightning fell. Skipper Gooseneck struck the bell once, and one of our Seamanship Instructors appeared from nowhere, as was his way. The Skipper lodged a complaint, and in a minute the guilty were told that if they were put in the Captain's Report for impertinence to the ferryman they would get not less than a month of black list, which was no light matter even in the summer half. Even the tough found a week of black list plenty. The passing for pirate suddenly lapsed. I am glad to be able to say that later in the term our men gave "Skipper Gooseneck" a handsome present of tobacco, so that all was quiet on the Potomac (for a time).

That evening, while I was drawing from memory the ships I had been aboard, a weather-beaten second-class P.O. came to look at my work. I had often noticed him in the morning cutter with Red Swab, and had been attracted by his look of charm, distinction, and weather-beatenness. He looked as if he had spent most of his life clawing off lee shores in gales of wind. I was still in the new chum's stage, of being awed by a senior's condescension in speaking to me, especially a morning cutter man. He said: "You take a fool's advice, chum, and draw all you can. Draw rigging whenever you get a chance; it will pay you more than you think. Very soon, now, there'll be exams; and in the seamanship exams you'll be asked to draw almost everything there is. Besides, if you draw a thing once, you'll know it always."

A rude and fierce mariner, who had stopped to listen, said: "That's right. I'm a —— sight better seaman than . . . or . . . any day; but I can't draw what I know, and they can. The result is, that they get rated, and I'm a —— maintopman still. It's a —— shame. A kid like this chum here will get rated before me, just because he can draw."

My weather-beaten friend said that of course, the exams were very unfair, and no real test of proficiency in seamanship. What was really needed was an exam, man by man, at a model mast, fitting the rigging, securing the spars, and sending up the yards. A dozen model masts, five or six feet over all, in the modern style, would jolly soon show who knew seamanship. The debate spread; soon half a dozen were sitting on my desk or form debating our defects. It was the opinion that it would be a very costly matter to put in a modern foremast, with all its gear and sails. "And of course, if you put in a modern foremast, you'll have to put in a modern spike jibboom; and then there's the question: will the ship stand it?" The wise ones said: "Yes, of course she would stand it. She was built to stand ninety guns, engines, and terrific masts. At most, it would be only putting iron knees and beams in the way of the shroud screws." We had not much knowledge of costs; we supposed that it would cost two thousand pounds. It seemed a good deal of money to men penniless after a day ashore. My weather-beaten friend said: "It may be too much money. But if it's too much money, they could get a dozen good model masts, with modern rigging and trusses for five pounds each. You only need the lower mast and topmast; it's all repeated up above. They could easily get the screws cut, and they'd last a long time. With a dozen of those, an examiner would see in five minutes which of a class knew anything; he could stop their grog according."

The pipe for clearing up decks broke the meeting. The weather-beaten man said that after a Liverpool Leave he did not want any supper, and suggested, to my amazement, that I should come and mooch. I was deeply honoured. We went on deck and mooched round, in the usual slouch, arm-in-arm. I asked him what a garboard strake was. He repeated the phrase; he did not know it. He called out to one or two of our primest seamen and asked them; they did not know it, and replied with ribaldry. He said that we would ask one of the Instructors as we went down.

My new friend said that it would be a disturbed night probably; so many men would be upset from all the varieties of tuck they had stowed away during the day. This was the case; a good many men, who had mixed their cakes or had no stomach for dainties, repented during the night, and vowed amendment next time.

I was attracted by this weather-beaten man. I

mooched with him a good deal, for the rest of the term, always very much as a disciple with a master; yet looking to have a few minutes walk with him either before breakfast, or before night Divisions. If I had any tuck, I shared it with him. He was a wise, quiet fellow. After his first voyage he came on board one Sunday, and dined in my mess. He died at sea many years ago. I remember him saying, that though the Horn was cold, a northerly winter gale in the Channel was the coldest cold he had ever known.

Going down that night we passed an Instructor. My friend hailed him and asked: "What is a garboard strake, please?" The man smiled and said: "What you mustn't put your foot through."

"Oh, any fool knows that; but what is it?"

"Why, the strake of plank next the keel in the bottom of a ship. You might call it the ship's bottom."

We spread this knowledge through the ship in due course.

Our Instructor had told me to look out for the Runcorn Fleet, in case it might contain a "two topsail schooner". I saw the Runcorn Fleet several times; a most wonderful sight it was; it made our matchless sea library complete, except for that "two topsail schooner", which I never saw.

On some fine, sunny day, with a fair E. or NE. wind, perhaps a hundred lovely things passed us under sail. Nothing of these was bigger than a barquentine (that most lovely rig), yet all of them bore the marks of an intense personal pride and affection. They were the homes of their masters; each showed his skill and care; each was a little masterpiece of seamanship. Most of them were topsail schooners, a few were brigantines, a few were two- or three-masted schooners; a good many were ketches or yawls; some were cutters. Among them, were odd rigs, such as one never saw elsewhere, and now cannot see at all. Among these were cutters with crossed yards, setting square sails. Once one came by with an odd triangular yardless topsail, then, very rare, but now in use again. We were told that it would be called a Jimmy Green if set above a royal, an Angel's Whisper if set above a skysail, and a Trust to God if set above a moonsail. I loved being aloft looking at these things. I was given the key to them, I was being taught their grammar and learning their language; half of our land's story was explained to me.

My chief delight was still the topmast rigging. It never failed to charm me. I loved the climb, and the improvement in the climb, the trotting, where once I had dragged; I could now trot up and dance down. Someone had once danced down into me and had kicked me in the mouth, with the effects foretold to me. It was often cold aloft, now. Like most new chums, I tried to be indifferent to cold; to go up to the cross-trees, and stay till half frozen seemed sailor-like and salt. Suddenly, there came a day, when the word went that we were to make all snug for the winter. Red Swab warned us that we should have a hard afternoon of it.

I took part in two other makings snug, and found them both easy, in the one I was working aloft; in the other, I knew what was being done, and delighted in it. This first time, I remember only as a very weary toil. The topmen leaped aloft at the order, in a way that made the heart beat. The sails came down in their gear; we had to bear them to the locker. The topgallant yards came spinning down as before, and were stopped into the shrouds. Then the topgallant masts came down; and we, who were running and pulling on deck, had to stow them away. Then the gear began to come down; we had to coil it, bundle it, label it, and bear its heavy, knobby, block-and-cringly weights down to deeps in the hold; never to any place where one could find a ship's cutlass, pistol, or tomahawk, from her old equipment. Nor was it possible for even the cleverest among us to linger in the hold, exploring; we were wanted for the work on deck, and driven to it. Lastly, the topsail yards were struck, and the three topmasts housed. We were now snug for the winter. For some reason, we were much longer at the work than on the later occasions. I was very tired at the end of the afternoon when we were piped to dress. If I had understood what each process meant, and had been encouraged to sing and shout while working, it would have been a jolly time. The instinct of boys is to sing and shout; the entire sailing Merchant Service always sang out at any work whatsoever. Whenever Nature drove us to cry aloud at work, we were always checked and told to be silent. The discipline was good, perhaps; if it made the routine leaden, it did not matter much, as we had almost always enough hands for every job.

I was shocked at the change in the ship's appearance when the topmasts were struck. I found, too, that going aloft was little fun, now that I could only go up into the top; it was better than nothing, of course, for there was nowhere else to go.

At about this time, one of the events of the half occurred. I never knew all the story, for the man concerned was much senior to me, and not in my watch.

I had sometimes seen, and had once had my eyes ——by, a certain tough man in the port watch. He was one of the weather-beaten salts, who had been in the ship a long time, and had not prospered. He was sick of the ship, and eager to get to sea. How he arranged it, and what he did, I never heard. The ship's version of it, later, was that he had been very clever.

I had not liked the man, but, then, we hardly knew each other; I knew him by sight and had had my eyes —— by him, that was all our shipmateship amounted to.

Going ashore on a half-holiday, with two fellow focslemen, we ran past the slip shop to avoid being pressed into pony service, and got into the Rock Park. We had had leave to go for a walk, and were conscious of innocence, yet all the same we were all three terrified, when suddenly the Skipper came tearing round a corner right on to us. We petrified to attention and took off our caps. He seemed to have been running, and all the storm signals were hoisted; we quaked. "You boys," he said, "how long have you been ashore?"

"Not two minutes, sir."

"Have you seen . . . ? (this salt of the port watch) since you came ashore?"

"No, sir."

"If you see him, my orders to you three are, that you drag him back on board by main force. Bring him back on board, at once. Do you understand?"

"Yes, sir."

"My orders are, that every member of the ship is to help you."

"Yes, sir."

He glared upon us, and went on, to give his orders to others. We proceeded on our walk, wondering what . . . had done, and supposing, that he had probably had his leave stopped by the Skipper that morning, had then watched the Skipper go ashore, had judged that he might risk it, and had taken leave. Anyhow, it was no part of a new chum's duty to lay violent hands on anybody outside the ship, and for us to lay hands on a senior, it might be magnificent, it was not sense; we were not yet tired of life. We went for our walk in peace.

. . . was not at muster after leave ended. He was not at mess later. He was never again seen by any of us. It was said, later, that he had in some way got himself aboard a ship bound to San Francisco. During the next half, we heard (I know not how truly), that he had arrived at San Francisco, and being of a roving turn, had gone ashore there. San Francisco was then a rousing romantic place, with a fairly tough sailor town called the Barbary Coast. . . . being ashore became a cowboy on a cattle ranch not far from the port, and getting into a dispute "with a Greaser" (so the story went), was killed by the Greaser. I sometimes wondered, if from force of habit he had —— the Greaser's eyes.

Many years later, being in San Francisco, I tried, without any success whatever, to learn something of the case: there was no record.

When I had been a while on board, I had an accident, which brought me to the Sick Bay. It was on a Saturday morning, during the general scrubbing. I was in sea boots, hurrying down the main hatch from the upper deck, and not knowing yet that soapy and some kinds of wet wood are slippery, even to new rubber sea boots. The main hatch was being scrubbed with soapy water; I slipped upon it on one of the top steps and came down for the rest of the double flight to the lower deck where I belonged. Before I could pick myself up, I was lifted by some admirable men and carried to the Sick Bay, where the Nurse asked where I was hurt. My leg was hurt. She ordered me to undress and get into bed; some pyjamas were brought to me; my leg was massaged with arnica; and I was left to look about me. The Nurse had a somewhat fierce way with mariners; perhaps it was as well.

There were two other patients in bed there; one,

rather far aft, with a bit of a temperature; the other with a sprained ankle, beside me, near the forward bulkhead. He was a senior, but only just so; from the starboard mizen. He began a conversation with me, and was silenced by the Nurse.

I saw on the bulkheads of the Bay two large oil paintings, representing the first and second *Conways*. Apart from these works of art there was nothing to beguile the mind. We watched the Nurse, who was busy cleaning the already spotless place. If we ventured any remark, we were silenced; if we asked any question we were snubbed. Red Swab called to have a look at me when he had finished with his deck. He said he would see that my washing went off, and my dinner brought down. I rashly said that I hoped to be on deck with the focsle next day. The Nurse told me at this that I should be back with the focsle *if she thought fit,* not unless. Red Swab managed to send me up some books to read. Then, presently, the morning was done; one of my mess brought down my dinner, and later removed the dishes. The Nurse took a grim inspection of us, withdrew to her cabin, and presently came out, dressed for the shore, to warn us not to be up to any pranks while she was out of the ship.

When we were pretty sure that the launch was away, we thought that we were out of all possible trouble until tea-time. In this we were wrong. Almost at once two men entered who made our bloods run cold. Both were seniors, one a second-class P.O., of whom I knew nothing, one way or the other; he was not in my watch and I had not come across him. The other, though not in my watch I had come across; he was the new chum's terror whose repeated sayings made us marvel that lightning did not strike him. These two, who had watched the Nurse ashore, now came in, made themselves comfortable in the easiest seats, and lighted cigarettes. They were going to smoke there. I judged at the time, that the P.O. had not gone ashore because of some duty; he may have been in charge of the dinghy, perhaps. The other, of course, had had his leave stopped.

I must say, that the terror's conversation, which detailed his plans for a part of the winter holidays, was appalling to me. He talked like John Silver's parrot; "passing belief for wickedness", and all the time his easy insolence, in sitting there, smoking, certain of no interruption, seemed the last word in knowledge of the world. I marvelled that he had not chosen the Skipper's office. They talked together (he did most of the talking) till they had had enough of talk and tobacco. He had detailed his wickeder schemes, confessed his grimier crimes, and advanced his more daring theories; now he rose, and suggested that they should give each patient a large dose of black draught. The big bottle of this mixture was there on the table, with the gargles and the cough mixture, the usual ship's medicines.

Of course, the suggestion was rapturously received by his companion; they advanced upon us; my neighbour said that he had sprained his ankle. "All right," he said, "a —— good dose of black draught will do you both good. In fact, it will be just the thing to prevent complication. Come on, now. A bumper each, and the toast: 'To Hell with Government'."

He had the big bottle, and hope seemed dim, when my neighbour, with great presence of mind, and splendidly a liar, said: "For God's sake no. We're full up with black draught already; we've both been dosed. Another dose will kill us." This was false, but it was so like the ship's medical routine that it was judged to be true. They looked at each other, and forebore. A second dose of the mixture might well have been fatal to the strongest, and they did a little shrink from murder. The bottle was replaced. Then they got the Nurse's duster and removed traces of cigarette ash, matches, and so forth. They opened up ports and door, to lessen the smell of smoke, and with great adroitness burned some brown paper and sprinkled a little disinfectant, to confuse the scents. They told us that if the Nurse said that we had been smoking we could call her a —— liar; with this, they withdrew. We breathed again.

I have called this man "the new chum's terror". The reader should remember that this is a partial and prejudiced view of him. It is likely, that to the seniors, his contemporaries, "good old Josh", or whatever term of endearment he went by, was the life and soul of the ship's company. He might even have been much surprised to hear that anyone thought him a terror. He was not eminent in the ship, as a scholar or a seaman; his great quality was activity. He was what we called "a smart hand".

In all exercises, and especially in all work aloft, he was conspicuously smart. In reefing topsails, he was always the weather ear-ring man, the man first up at the yardarm, and often the first down, too, by way of the backstays. In furling, he was the man in the bunt who made the beautiful cone with the wrinkleless skin. This smartness was unusual, and very much admired by us and by our officers. He must have been frequently on the report and in the black list, but this reckless sailor-like activity always warmed the officers' hearts to him; he was forgiven much. He did well at sea, of course.

I was dismissed from the Sick Bay the next morning; I was very glad to escape. Later I saw something of the sprained ankle case. I was able to thank him for his ready lie about the black draught. It was he who first taught me that a necessary part of my life was the care of my clothes. Our uniforms were subject to a good many strains to which clothes are not usually subject. In the doing of much rough work daily, pumping, hauling, scrubbing, etc., strains came upon buttons and joins. We tended to lose trouser buttons, and part at seams. Finding that I was running short of trouser buttons, my new friend showed me what to do. I had never before attempted to put on a button or make even the simplest mend. Now I was shown how to look after myself a little. We each had a housewife, with needles, thread, scissors, etc., as a part of our gear. In each housewife was a box of patent trouser-buttons with studs. These had been chosen, perhaps, as easier to boys than the usual sew-on button. My friend showed me how to bore a hole in the trouser, for the insertion of the stud, and then how to press the button on to the stud. Suddenly, with a click, the button fixed itself upon the stud, never to come off again. Going further my friend showed me how very important it was to take stitches in time. Going aloft made trousers split at the fork seam; hauling made tunics go at the armpit. He showed me how to thread a needle and sew some strong preventive stitches at these points. I will not say that I was clever at this; I got into the way of doing it, and later added to it some rough parody of the art of darning. These simple accomplishments have been of much use to me in my pilgrimage; all boys should be taught to wash and mend their clothes.

My sewing teacher used to make a good deal of money by sewing pockets into the trousers of his shipmates. We were allowed only one pocket (in the tunic) by regulation; and this was short measure, for boys. My teacher was highly skilled in making effective trouser pockets out of our regulation blue handkerchiefs.

He was friendly to me. Later, he went to sea in a ship which was wrecked (without loss of life). I was told, long afterwards, I know not with what truth, that he did well at sea, and received an appointment to some ship; a good appointment. By several small accidents he was kept from joining her; she sailed with someone in his place and was lost with all hands.

At the end of October, a man told me that on the morrow there would be the first sign of holidays. On the first of November, it was possible to say that we should be going home next month. On turning out, he said, the C.P.O. will call for three cheers for going home next month; and everybody will cheer like mad. Later, he added, "we cheer for going home in six weeks, five weeks, four weeks, at the beginning of each week, but we don't cheer much till the last week, when we cheer every day, and make as much noise as we can". This was something to look forward to all day.

Sure enough, when the pipe called all hands next morning, the C.P.O. from his nook in the Stranger's Galley (as the port main on the orlop deck was then called), called out in his somewhat husky voice: "Three Cheers for Going Home next Month." We cheered our best. Long afterwards, I learned that our early morning cheers were heard in what was called The Dingle, where Matthew Arnold had lately lived. People there heard us, and wondered why we made such joy so early in the day.

By this time I had begun to find my feet a little. I no longer dreaded my hammock. I could lash and carry fairly well. I could polish my shoes; I did all the work given me willingly and fairly well. I knew everybody on board by sight and reputation, even if they were in the other watch. I had begun to distinguish the pipes. At any rate, I was now sure, that if the pipe blew briefly and shrilly, and the order sounded like YOW, YOW, it would not concern me. If the pipe were a little more than a blast, if it tended to become two blasts, and the following order sounded like YOW, YOW, jabber-jabber-jee, then, it would be wiser for me to ask an older hand what the pipe was. Of course, the Pipe Down, the All Hands (in the early morning) and the Pipe to Dinner were unmistakable. I learned too, that the Yow Yow Pipes would concern me in my next term.

Directly after dinner on Sundays, most of us pulled out desks, brought up our ink-pots and writing cases, and wrote our letters. The ship was always very quiet on Sundays, and much emptier than usual, since week-end leave was rather freely given then, to men with friends in the district. The writers sat under the eye of the P.O. who had the main deck watch that day. After the feast of our Sunday dinner even the tigers in our company were disposed to be benign; the P.O.'s task of keeping order was nominal; still, he had to be there.

Towards the end of the term on a November Sunday, I was writing at one of the main deck desks, when I saw the P.O. of the deck, with a little pack of books in his hand, moving from group to group on the port side, chatting with friends, or looking at a drawing. I had often seen him before, and knew him to be a prodigy of learning, of strength and nautical skill, who had won I knew not how many prizes the term before. He was a first-class P.O. with broad gold stripes to his sleeves.

He was one of the Quarter Boys, due to leave at the end of the term. Like most of the men on board, he had several nick-names, the one given when he was a new chum, the one given by the ship when it had grown accustomed to him, and the one or two used by his familiar friends. I had heard him called a ribald name, and "Skysail", and "S.H.", his usual name, which stood for "Smart Hand". He was a very smart hand, one of our smartest, but he was much more, he was a fine natural seaman, well able to do ticklish jobs on the rigging, from wire splicing to any kind of a mat. He had a name for being able to understand Compass Deviation at a first reading; anyhow, he struck a kind of awe into a new chum.

Presently, he came across to my desk. I had never spoken to him, of course, now he spoke to me. "Is anybody sitting here, chum?" I said: "No." He took place beside me, and disposed his books for study. He took the place solely because it gave him a good view of the deck: it was very important to me. The book he read was a novel called *Euthanasia;* one of the books set aside was a red volume by R. H. Scott, called *Meteorology*. I saw the title, and supposed that it must be a book about shooting stars and comets. It lured me to it, for I had seen some fine shooting stars not many nights before, and longed to know about them. When I had finished my writing, I plucked up my courage. He looked a nice chap; he had always seemed a nice chap, he had the name of being a first-rate sort of chap; so I boldly asked if he would mind my looking at his book. Now there were some seniors who would have answered my request with a stock phrase. "If you've not got a blasted neck", an expression with more effect than meaning; or, as Dr. Johnson would have said, "gross, ignorant and disrepectful".

But, mark now, he *was* a nice chap. He smiled upon me. "Why, of course," he said, "have you done any Meteorology?"

"No; none; I'm afraid I don't know what it is."

"Weather," he said. "Laws of Storms and that sort of thing." He looked at me, and seemed to discern an eagerness for knowledge in me. "You'd better begin at a place which may interest you," he said. He turned to an admirable account of the passing of a typical depression "very slow in coming on". "That is one of the best things," he said. I took the Scott; he returned to *Euthanasia*. I was disappointed that the book was not about meteors; still, weather was pretty good. I had always read that sailors were very good at weather, and could foretell it for days ahead; possibly, I could learn to do this.

As I read, the subject became more interesting than I had supposed possible; it became so much bigger; I found that weather did not depend on caprice, but on enormous forces; and though this was knowledge, it was delightful to me; I wanted to know more of it. From time to time my companion put down his novel to have a look at his deck, which was quiet enough, except for men perhaps asking if anyone had a stamp to spare. "How are you getting on?" he asked.

"It's very interesting."

"Yes; isn't it?" Again, he looked at me, with a smile, that a new chum should care about knowledge. "Can you tell the weather?" he asked.

"No. I'm afraid I can't. I suppose you can?"

"O yes, with a very good barometer."

He soon laid aside his book to make the tour of his deck, and chat with friends; he was a very popular man. When he came back, it was time to clear up decks. He said: "Chum, if you're interested in weather, come along and mooch."

We went on deck to mooch, with linked arms, in the usual slouch. I was amazed at his condescension, so were some of his contemporaries, who called out: "Your spare new chum," and other ribaldry. It was coming to be a flaming sunset; one of the old Instructors was looking at the sky. He quoted the couplet:

"A mackerel sky, with mare's tails,
Makes a lofty ship carry low sails."

My friend said to me: "Remember that, and remember that it is not always true. And remember, that the upper clouds are very little known, and that by watching them all the time, we may get to know something. What makes you interested in weather?"

"You do."

He was pleased by this. "All right," he said, "I'm

keeping the Log at present. If you like you shall help."
Did I like to help, "to help", a mixture of Phœbus
Apollo, Leonardo da Vinci, Sophocles, Sir Isaac Newton and Captain Cook? He showed me how to read a
mercurial barometer, how to take the wet and dry
bulbs, how to draw a bucket of water for the spec-grav
readings. (I had learned how to draw water, but to
draw it for him, for this purpose, was a new matter; it
was a joy to do it for him.) He taught me the different
sorts of clouds, and roughly what each meant. He persuaded me to watch the upper clouds for him, and to
observe the directions of their drifts. Sometimes, I had
the extraordinary interest of doing these things with
him.

The privilege of doing these things for him and with
him was enchantment to me. Then, in the nick of
happy time, a kind friend sent me a pound of butter. I
had learned to be a little cautious about tuck. I did not
tell the world, now, that I had some tuck; no, I put the
butter in my chest with my sea boots, where people
would not be likely to look for butter. But I learned
that my new friend loved having bread and butter at
dinner, when the ship supplied neither; so, while the
butter lasted, I brought him some for dinner, each day.
One could always lay in a store of bread at breakfast. I
used to take an extra "share" at breakfast, that is, about
an eighth part of a big loaf. Tucking this into my tunic,
I took it to my chest, where with a jack-knife I gouged
a hole in the crumb, filled the hole with a blob of but-

ter, and stopped the hole with the crumb again. I did this privily, when men were not about; then, at dinner, I could hurry to the godlike being's mess, and hand him the salted gold-mine of the share of bread.

He was the first to give me a real delight in study, and I think that he was pleased to find me so eager a pupil. He said that all officers ought to know the sciences which related to the sea, and that there were not nearly enough keen observers. He said that men who kept careful notes all the time were often of real help to the Meteorological Office, who sometimes rewarded good observers with sets of wonderful instruments.

I asked him what name I was to call him; which would be permitted; he said: "Bill."

" 'Bill, Bill', he said, 'or words to that effect.' "

I asked him if he knew yet what ship he was sailing in? He told me, "yes", and that he would be sailing in her, probably in the coming February. He showed me in his setting-in book a little painting of her, done from her sail plan by our best water-colour painter. It struck me as an exquisite painting of a clipper ship. She was of about one thousand, four hundred tons, I judge, fully rigged, and, as I saw with my own eyes later, very beautiful. She was painted steel grey, with masts and yards of the dull yellow "mast colour". She was elegant in the choicest English style, and being almost new had all the latest sailors' blessings; nothing above her royals, double topgallant yards, a spike jib boom and no spanker gaff. She had a donkey engine, deck capstans and fiferail winches for the braces. You could see at a glance that a lot of thought and love had gone to her building and fitting; she was a work of art, sure to draw men's hearts wherever she came.

He sailed in her early in the next term, on one of our half-holidays. By a miracle of kindness, the Chief gave me leave to go to Pierhead to try to see her sail, instead of going to the Baths. Such leave was very rarely granted, and would never have been given to me had not the Chief admired Bill as much as I did.

I knew enough of the time of high water, when she would sail, to know that I had no great chance of seeing her; just the bare chance. You will know how boyhood longs for a thing; I longed to be at Pierhead in time, to see Bill in blue dungarees, and to shout: "So long Bill. Good luck," and to see him grin, and hear him say something rude and friendly. While on my way in the ferry, I could see his ship's masts, and knew them by the Blue Peter. I could see that she was headed for the River, but not yet moving. When the ferry reached the Stage, I leaped and ran, as I never, never ran for the Baths. I was never a fast runner, but I could keep on for a long time, and this time I went all out; I very nearly did it.

Not quite, though. When I came within sight of her, she was passing through the dock gates into the river. I was just in time to hear the Pierhead give her three cheers as she passed out, and her crew reply with three more. She was in the River in an instant, more than a

hundred yards from me. I saw her new Red Ensign, her
house-flag, and Blue Peter; then the warehouse roofs
hid her. The little gang of Pierhead, a few sad women,
some boarding-house runners, crimps, ships' chandlers,
dock labourers, riggers, and outward-bound-looking
seamen, who had gone there for the jump, broke up,
and came back towards me. I asked one of them, if I
could get back to the Stage by a way upon my right. He
said I could. I set off running to get back to the Stage
before her tug had plucked her past; and though I was
held up at one of the swing bridges, which then broke
the streams of traffic there, I saw her pass with her tug;
I knew the tug well, and never saw her afterwards without emotion.

There is something indescribably beautiful about
the motion of a fine ship with a tug in a fairway. She
herself is often looking her best for the occasion, she is
looking beautiful with power at rest, the tug is looking
resolute with power in being. The sun shone, the water
rushed and flung sprays about, the gulls dipped and
wavered. She drew past with a kind of thoughtful saun-
ter, as though none of all this mattered, she would
presently take wing. She was a very beautiful ship, with
the bows, and sheer and exquisite elliptic stern which
always laid me low with their beauty. I used to quake
at the thought that men could make those lines out of
iron hacked out of earth with pick axes.

She was going pretty fast; I ran along the Stage
parallel with her as far as I could go. Her crew probably

lay blind drunk in the focsles. Her mates and apprentices were busy about her decks; I knew that Bill was
one of them; I had no glass and could not tell which was
he. I waved my blue handkerchief in the intervals of
running, and wished Bill all manner of good luck. Presently, she dimmed into the haze of the lower River;
there was nothing for it but to run back.

Some twenty months later, before I left the ship, Bill
was back in Liverpool and came on board. To my surprise and pleasure, he remembered me, and sought me
out. I had no bread and butter for him, but I was then
captain of a mess and could invite him to dinner in my
mess, which I did. We had a very happy time, talking
about the weather and other matters. He was even
burlier than he had been, the sea agreed with him; he
liked it, but was very critical of our methods which he
judged to be not those of wisdom, nor of commonsense.

I was very happy to see him again, and hoped that we
might meet again some time. We never did; after that
day, I neither saw him nor heard of him. I had expected
that he would become famous; he did not. I had supposed that as a member of our peculiar community, I
should always be able to find out what became of him
and where he was. Usually, we could trace the doings
and the whereabouts of our men; our nets spread all
over the world; we could find out. Yet, with three men
of my time, this has not been possible; no man knows
what became of them; Bill was one of the three, and the
only one that mattered. Well . . . the sailing ship sea

was a fairly fatal water, which took a good many young men; I suppose it took Bill, and somehow the word never reached us. It did not take his ship; she lived to a great age, for a sailing ship, and died a natural death at last in a ship-breaker's yard.

I have a photograph of Bill, and another of his ship; the two made a pair; splendid creatures both, and parts of me while memory lasts.

Had I asked earlier, I might have heard of Bill. There was this against it; he sailed alone, without other men from our company; then, for a good many years life to myself was perplexing and full, and I happened to meet few seamen.

In the dark autumn evenings, when there were no school classes, my friend the Second Officer, sometimes broke up our painting by a loathsome thing called Small Arm Party. The pipe would go for all hands to fall in on the lower deck; we would fall in; and being all present he would pick some eighty of us, and drill us for an hour. Sometimes, we had to march to the Armoury for rifles and cutlasses. We never drew the cutlasses, only girded them on like the minstrel boy (magnificent of course, but not war). If we had drawn them we should have notched the woodwork somewhat.

In the November of that half, the Captain urged us to study chess. Our headmaster was an expert and scholar in the games of draughts and chess. His library was said to consist of books on these games. I judge that it was he who suggested chess to the Skipper. One evening, after prayers, the Skipper told us that he would give a prize to the ship's chess champion, if we would organize a tournament.

There were not many chess players among us; still, enough came forward to make a tournament, and lots were drawn for the rounds. I was drawn to play the first game and felt that now the focsle would see what sort of a star their 35 was. My supporters came with me to the library, and the contest began. Unfortunately, the Skipper came down to give distinction to the occasion; and his presence made me quake with stage fright. My opponent was a big fellow, of great uprightness and goodness of heart; three years older than myself and one of the best brains on board. He grinned at me with his wonderful array of teeth as though he were just a little sorry that now he had to proceed to eat me. This he soon did, of course. Black (I was Black) resigned at the nineteenth move. By the end of the second evening White had crumpled all his other opponents with similar ease, and won the prize. It was worth the pain, though: White was always very friendly to me, later.

The ship's custom in all mattters was to ask for what you wanted. If a man wanted something to read, he went about asking people for it, till he either got a book or a clout over the head to keep him quiet. I had learned at once as a new chum not to go for anything whatever into certain quarters; new chums were not allowed there. As the term went on, and confidence grew, I learned that I could go to some places. I could

go borrowing over about half the orlop deck. Books
were not common among my shipmates; our chests
were our only storage room, and our kits filled these.
The most plentiful books were old nautical novels by
Captains Marryat, Chamier and Glascock. Of these,
Marryat was the most frequent and very much the best;
most of his books were to be had there. I found more
joy in them than most boys, because I was living in a
society such as he describes, and the setting was the one
about me. My chest was now under a port. In my spare
time, when I wished to read, I would come down to my
chest, open it, and sit on my folded rug. By dismantling
the lid chains, a chest could be made as easy as a deck
chair. I had but to lift my eyes, or go up a hatchway,
and there would be Mr. Chucks, Frank Mildmay,
Vigors, Martin, and the excellent Swinburne; very
likely all together, just as Marryat made them. Then,
somebody lent me *Oliver Twist*, with the awful drawing of Fagin in the condemned cell. I read this with an
intense delight. I did not begin upon the later Dickens'
books until more than a year later.

Those who were hard up, had a way of trying to raise
the wind by selling their belongings, going from chest
to chest, with the articles, asking man after man, if he
would like to buy. The very hard up used to try to sell
parts of their kit; trousers, tunics, uniform caps, fetch
bags, etc. They got wretched prices for these, if they
ever sold them. I have seen one bold sprig trying to sell
a tunic. "A —— fine go-ashore tunic. Come on, now,

. . . Half-a-crown for a tunic. You won't give half-a-crown. Two bob, then. . . . Two bob for a tunic. Two bob or overboard.'' Then, as no one bid his price, the tunic went overboard, through the open port. On one fortunate day for me, a young man came round selling books, *Newton Forster,* which I had read, and *The Adventures of Huckleberry Finn,* with the old illustrations. Sixpence made these treasures mine. I had never read *Huck Finn,* but I must have read it at least once in every year since then, as I have read *Peter Simple, Treasure Island* and *Frank Mildmay the Naval Lieutenant.* I know not which of them gave me the most delight. I cannot read them today without some ghost of the old original joy coming back to me, in a memory of the scene, the old orlop deck, with the lines of chests, some men sitting in them, others changing clothes, or hanging round some whistler or fiddler, or playing the fool in some way, or tormenting a new chum who was ass enough to mind, or netting, or perhaps doing a neat job in seamanship, strop, point or becket, or mending a trouser crutch, or only passing by, calling: "Top, please."

In my asking for books, I was sometimes told: "I've only got a Blood." Stocks of Bloods could always be seen in a shop in Rock Ferry, and in many little shops in Liverpool. They were short romances, of small, thin, square, squat appearance, each with a stirring cover, usually, perhaps, of some Red or Black Avenger, printed in colours, doing something desperate with a cutlass, a pistol or a powder barrel. In my memory, they ran to about ten thousand words apiece, and in nearly every case, each was but a chapter in the life of the hero, so that the reader might be lured into buying the next instalment. Some of the covers drew the youthful, nautical eye with pictures of ships under the Jolly Roger, victims walking the plank, and these Byronic Avengers, above all human fraility, really getting their own back on the seniors. Those were still the days, too,

"When old Sitting Bull and Comanche Bills,
  Might lift off your scalp in the Dreary Black Hills."

Some Bloods dealt with Red Indians, Texan Rangers, Greasers, and cattle rustlers. These had covers representing cowboys stuck about with revolvers, or shot through with Indian arrows, yet still bearing the white maiden to safety upon the faithful mustang. To myself who, from childhood, had adored Captain Mayne Reid, these covers attracted even more than the Avengers. As I was told that some Bloods were exciting I bought two or three for myself; each volume cost only a penny. I may have chanced on a bad set, but mine were not worth the money; they were rubbish. After this, I bought no more: I laid out my pennies more wisely, on Italian Cream. I remember that one character in one of them said that "to live in Texas a man must be quick on the draw". I thought of this when I travelled in Texas many years later. It was no longer true; men were living there very well, without drawing anything, except, I hope, dividends, from virtue.

Somebody told me that I ought to know the stars. The wise friend in the morning cutter said that I ought not to spend my money on Italian Cream, in the way I did, but save it up till I could buy a Star Atlas. As this would have taken me a year, and flesh was boyish, he thought of another way. He borrowed a Star Atlas from a senior, got some stiff black paper somehow, and then helped me to make the most enchanting constellations with a sail needle. We would select some nice-looking constellation, Plough, or Pegasus, Cassiopeia and the Guards, or Orion, and then, by judicious jabs of the needle, prick it out on a black page. Then, holding the result up to the light, lo, there was midnight, with the stars shining in it, in their proper magnitudes.

Then, on a "dark night with a clear atmosphere" we would go upon the focsle head and pick out some other constellation for future drawing. We would see the shooting stars in their glory and the planets in their peace; and if these were not beauty enough, sometimes we had the moon, and always the River.

Fairly early in my time aboard, I was marched, with a landing party, to the funeral of someone associated with the ship. I have a dim memory of going to Bebbington, and of singing on the march back the indelicate song which had so won the fancy of the ship's company. Later in the term, one of the ship's managing Committee died. Red Swab told us about him at mess, how good a fellow he had been, and how merry a speaker on public occasions. A very large landing party was picked to attend this funeral; I was again picked; and away we went.

It was a bitterly cold, grey wintry day, overcast, and probably with a falling barometer. We marched in our best go-ashore uniforms, with nothing over our tunics. In fact, very few of us owned the pilot jacket overcoats prescribed as uniform; we so seldom needed them. While we were marching, with the wind behind us, we did not feel cold. When we reached the high-lying graveyard, and stood to attention waiting, it was another matter. It was no doubt evil weather at sea; a good many gulls were cruising over the cemetery, and pellets of snow drifted about. We grew colder and colder waiting; there was nothing for it, save to endure. I have been colder since then and have many times set myself to endure cold. Boys as a rule endure cold badly. Most of us suffered in that graveyard. It was not a cheerful occasion, and half of us faced the wind. When all was over, as we judged, when we were hoping for a quick march away, another ship's company, whose members looked far colder than we did, went in slow march to the graveside and there began and slowly sang through, unaccompanied, a long, dolorous funeral hymn, which I thought would never come to an end. Their faces looked blue, their noses snuffly, and their voices were all on edge. They got a kind of whine into it; they looked so like unhappy dogs howling that our hearts pitied them. They ended at last; and it fell to us to get out of the way. The excellent William Tozer saw clearly the state in which we were; he marched us out of the cemetery, and as soon as we were clear of the gates bade us double, which we did with joy, till we were warm again.

When we had lapsed to quick step, we were under the P.O.'s, some of whom started singing. Not all of us sang; there were pirates among us, who were thinking of the tuck shop on the slip. The seniors behind the ranks of new chums kept asking us, man by man, if we had any money, and bidding us fork it out, so that they might lay it out for us (as they said), to the best advantage. We had learned a little sense by this time; we denied the possession of money; though with sinking hearts, for we knew, that having pleaded poverty we should not be able to enter the tuck shop as we had hoped and planned. We should have to go without; well, that was better than seeing our Italian Cream go down the throats of enemies.

To most of us new chums, the slip shop or tuck shop was only to be entered when it was certain to be almost empty of seniors. It was a little place, and seniors hated being crowded; they liked to take their ease at their inn. But after half term or so, most new chums had peeped in at least, made a shy purchase, and fled away to share it with a chum. They had seen its shelves of joys, its double counter; its stacks of boxes of ginger-beer bottles, and the screens pencilled over with witty comments upon members of our ships' company. I had been in; I had bought Italian Cream; and had marvelled at the neatness of some of the satirical remarks. I had not dared to linger there; and now, as our party reached its lighted window, and the seniors fell out, we juniors went on down the slip to the boats in the cold. The boats' crews —— our eyes for not having any tuck for the boats' crews. It was coming on to be bad weather, wind and sea were rising; we were all glad to be aboard, out of it.

The indelicate song continued to solace the ship's company all through that term. The words must often have been audible in the Quarters, for on fine nights it was sung over and over again by a hundred singers at least, marching to its tune round the upper deck. No one was rebuked for it; probably our officers felt that the more we sang it, the sooner we should be sick of it, and that anyhow it would soon be supplanted. It held our hearts that term; the next term it gave way to two music-hall songs, then being performed with success by Miss Collins and Mr. Chevalier. Some of our daring spirits during that term sang *Sam Hall,* which I then heard for the first time. It had a flavour of the pit about it which won the reckless. Many other snatches of old song went round the deck in mooching times. Now that I call them to mind, they seem to have come from many quarters and many times. Among the sea songs, the most popular was *Spanish Ladies;* and next to this *Blow, ye winds;* and a mid-Victorian halliard song,

While cruising. These were often supplanted by chanties recently overheard from some neighbouring ship. I remember one crowd getting an anchor near us to *Rio Grande* and this set us all to *Rio Grande* for a fortnight. From the West, we had the Canadian Boating Song; from the East:

> "Laugh-ee, chaff-ee, plenty pidgin,
> Play-ee tum-tum all-ee day."

and from still further east, a song (quoted in a lecture on China) which took the ship's fancy for a while:

> "Ching-a-ring a-ring-ching: Feast of Lanterns,
> What a crop of chopsticks, hongs and gongs."

Youth takes kindly to all the arts, as parts of the play of youth. Though I was little, I felt at once, on coming aboard, that songs and painting were in their proper place, parts of life, precious to life, never-failing joys when life became bleak. We were going into a life in which everybody had to do decorative painting, and in which song of some sort was almost the only solace.

Perhaps, too, those were the days of song. The music-hall was at its perfection then, and comic, sentimental, rousing, and sometimes very charming songs were put into the popular heart by artists of rare talent, most of whom, I suppose, tried a new song each quarter, if not in each month. We had all these, of course. Those of our crew who came from cities taught us a new repertory at the beginning of each term.

New Chum

When the autumn had set in, a new delight was given on one evening of each week; a dancing class. The swinging lamps were shifted well out of the way of dancers' heads; the screens were lowered, to shut away the after end of the main deck; and the launch (or the cutter) made a late run for the dancing master. He was a little limber man, like a light-weight boxer. He must have been one of the last, I suppose, to use a kit fiddle. He taught those who wished, to waltz and to polka; sometimes a lady appeared, to play the piano, and sometimes even to dance with the more advanced. Full of joy, were those evenings of the dance; all were cheered by them; even those who sat to mock were sweetened by the music, and lifted by the rhythms to happier sarcasms than they could have reached un-aided. The dance sometimes had thirty couples mov-ing. All noise, all music, was made intense between deck and beams. The piano, or the little fiddle, mixed with the beat of the many feet with effects of strange beauty. The master always played a certain tune for his polka: *She's a pretty girl, rather;* and danced it alone with us as he played it. We had to partner ourselves; but it was all great fun, and many of us would have danced all night. Whatever faults there were among us, we all liked men who were good at their work; and all hands knew this little master to be good. He, and the lady, his assistant, brought delight with them and were respected. Later in my time, I sometimes helped to row them ashore in a late run in the cutter; and could never

253

see them pass away into the darkness without the thought that they had come from fairyland, where dancers dwell, and were now going back into fairyland, having left with us the memories of music and rhythm, which we should never forget.

Sometimes, when teachers, speakers and visitors were not well liked, the cutters' crews would souse them well. That was never done to these bringers of the dance to mortals; no late run, even in bad weather, was ever grudged to them. Surely all the generosities of the soul come from the arts; and they alone bring life.

In spite of this occasional happy dancing, in the cold and dark of the long November evenings, there was often a great deal of boredom. When the boats were hoisted, or moored at the boom, there might be a long freedom between tea and supper, with no work, and no great chance of amusement. In the free evenings, some boxed, fenced, read or drew, but these delights seldom filled the whole time, nor engaged everybody. Perhaps it was to check the boredom, that the Small Arm Parties were devised; on the whole, I judged that they increased it, for few found any amusement in them; and they made the men feel that they could not call the free time free.

The men were glad of the freedom, up to a point; they were glad to be quit of the severe mental grinding of usual school routines, which stretch growing boys more than is wise. But a ship is a constricted space and always under discipline; if it were wet, so that we could not mooch on the 'upper deck, we had no place for noise; and there is an instinct towards noise, and to rebellion against quiet, in lively youth, in health.

It was late in this November, that a rebellion against quiet began among the most trusted of the senior P.O.'s. Under the leadership of the C.P.O. and the Captain of the Hold, a party was formed, calling itself The Good Cause League. Its members were mostly Quarter Boys, who expected to leave the ship in a few weeks; their object was to do as much damage as they could to ship's property. I suppose that the league contained only about half a dozen members, with, perhaps, half a dozen active sympathizers among a body called The Pirate's Crew, a wicked and fully budded growth which did not really flower till the new year. As a new chum, I knew nothing of the existence of the league, nor dreamed of its possibility, till, going on deck one day, I found one of the Instructors looking at the barge's falls which had been cut. Of course, the barge was secure with gripes and life-lines, still the cuts had been made, and if the cutter had cut the gripes and life-lines first, the barge which looked so fine on Sundays, would have come down with a run. Of course, it would have been hard for any cutter to cut gripes and life-lines unobserved from somewhere. There was always a P.O. in charge of the upper deck; he had noticed nothing unusual or suspicious during the time of the cutting of the falls. On a dark night, to cut the falls at the cleats was easy and simple. If the officer of the deck were forward or on the starboard side he could not possibly see the cleats; the criminal had simply to wait, with the knyf hid under his cloke, till the officer had passed forward or to starboard; a few steps took him to the cleats, a few seconds sufficed for the cuttings, and a few steps more brought the wicked one to safety. On a dark night, the chances of the man being caught cutting falls or other gear on the upper deck were small.

It was enquired into, of course; we were asked, what we knew about it; nobody seemed to know anything about it; and as no great harm had been done no great pressure was brought upon the ship's company, to discover the criminal. Then, in a day or two, the destruction of property became serious; other ropes were cut; the wet and dry bulbs were smashed in their case; brooms disappeared from their racks and were seen no more; swabs, scrubbers and buckets went from the manger; rudders, tillers, stretchers and oars from boats. It was clear, that some of these things could only have gone through the negligence or wilful blindness of petty officers on duty.

As the losses were noticed and reported at once, the enquiry was prompt. The Skipper sent for some senior petty officers, among whom were the chief members of the conspiracy. If they had been shrewder, they might have kept the matter secret until the end of term, when they would have left the ship for ever. They had but to promise every endeavour to find the guilty ones, and then to lie low, doing, perhaps, no more damage till the last night of term, when a large body of thoughtless youth would perhaps have borne a hand in the mischief. Then, after a really gaudy night. . . . But one of the conspirators had a grudge against a very fine fellow, to whom most of us were devoted. The grudge was an old one, shared by several bad men of the same term, and as they were nearly two years senior to me I have no notion of what the quarrel was: it had lasted a long time, and must have been very bitter. I am, however, certain that they were the men to blame in the dispute; the other man's face, character and record spoke for themselves. The conspirators had the baseness to charge this fine fellow with the crimes of the gangsters; and this accusation led directly to the accuser's downfall. Our fine fellow was at once cleared; the delator by a rash reply told much more than he meant to tell; and very soon all the members of the Good Cause League were on the report, and rather more.

Suddenly, two or three senior petty officers were seen standing on the quarterdeck, with looks of misery and despair. They had been eminent in the ship only the day before; now they were stripped of gold lace, buttons and badges; they were dressed in serges; sheer hulks were these poor Tom Bowlines; no longer darlings, nor members of our crew; they had been expelled and were waiting to be sent ashore. Each of them had forfeited a year's sea-time; the weight of that was to press upon them later; at the moment, they felt the falling out of our fellowship; we were all in fellowships there, after our first terms, and the bonds were close. These two or three left us. The less guilty members of the Good Cause League were (as I judge) pretty roughly spoken to, and put upon the black list till the end of term. On the black list, men said farewell to fun; they wore their jumpers; they turned out at half-past five or so; they ate their meals standing up on the quarterdeck: and did any unpleasant jobs of scraping, painting, etc., which marine ingenuity (a pretty clever sort) could devise for them. Any leisure from the jobs was passed on the quarterdeck, standing still, unspeaking and unspoken to, under the almost constant eye of the Officer of the Day.

However, term was drawing to an end; and some of these leaguers gave trouble later, in other terms.

As few men stayed on board for more than two years, the memory of the events of our life tended to be brief. We read certain names on the Prize Boards and remembered them; their doings were forgotten among us. We knew very little of what had happened in the ship more than two years before our own day. The Good Cause League, however, made an impression and became something of a legend. I heard men on board talking of it nine years afterwards.

Soon after the disruption of the Good Cause League, examinations wound up the work of the term. In the seamanship examinations, I found that even my rudimentary skill in drawing marine objects gave me an advantage. This was pointed out to me with bitterness by men who were better seamen than myself. I agreed with them; that examination should have been practical and done before the examining officer, with six-foot model masts.

We had been cheering the approaching holidays, week by week, on turning out in the mornings; we were expecting to go home about December 20th. Suddenly an epidemic of colds struck the ship's company, and the term was brought to an end. We were a week earlier in getting away. We had good notice of this, for I well remember the thrill throughout the ship when we began to cheer day by day, instead of week by week, during the last seven days. It always gave me a pang to hear the C.P.O. call for the cheers. The C.P.O. with the husky voice who had begun the cheering on November 1st had been sent out of the ship; he had not lived among us to taste the joy of the later cheering. His place was taken by another. Presently, an official came aboard with each man's railway ticket; and why these were not all lost, when each man had but one pocket for all purposes, is strange, indeed; some of them *were* lost. Then there came the unbelievable day, when we cheered for going home "tomorrow" and outdid ourselves in noise. Immediately after breakfast on this day, all men went down to the orlop deck, roused out their chest lashings, and lashed up each chest for going ashore. We were given labels and chalk, with which we had to make it utterly clear to which great railway station the chest was to be taken. We made these points clear beyond any possibility of error; then slides were rigged at the hatches, and with cheers and joy we raced our chests to the feet of ladders, hooked on the whips, and with more cheers men hove them up to the decks above and raced them along to the gangways. It was one of the best moments in any term, when the orlop deck was full of cheering gangs dragging and shoving at chests, colliding with other chests, hooking two or three together for the one hoist, and shouting to see them clash and scrape on the way up. The total weight shifted must sometimes have been several tons; they did not feel like tons at that end of a term. We soon cleared the orlop deck of them; the men above soon got them out of the ship, heaped them into the launch, the pinnace and empty, towed cutters. A few trips had them all ashore. What became of them, then; we never asked; but by some miracle of direction and order they were always at our stations when we came to claim them the next morning.

Usually, on the last night of the autumn term, a dance was given on board, on the lower deck, which was probably the best dancing floor within the kingdom. It fell to us to prepare it for the dancers by scattering French chalk, and then sliding up and down the deck till it was as slippery as good ice. I assure you, we prepared it. That hard, splinterless wood darkened under our polishing, and many came to know how hard it was before we had finished with it. We were all happily busy all day long with the fitting of the lower deck for the dancers, and of the main deck for the supper. The tables of the messes were supported lengthways along the deck, for ourselves, and athwartships, aft, for the guests. At dark, both these decks were hung with festoons of flags; a band came aboard, and took station between the old cannon at the foot of the main hatch. Great coloured Chinese lanterns were hung about both decks before the guests arrived; when these were lighted, the scene was strangely beautiful, like an underground fairyland. The guests came aboard in a ferry boat; they must have enjoyed their time, for the deck was a faultless floor, and our Captain, and his wife and daughters, the most welcoming, charming hosts. To us, the chief joy of the evening was the supper. To myself, there was always a special, strange pleasure, hard to describe, in seeing our decks full of people. The lowness of the beams in some way heightened the sense of life, much as it gave resonance to sound; then, the colour of the lights and dresses, the grace of the dance, and the power of the design which shrined us, the old line-of-battle-ship, all these things, together, pierced me to the core. Presently, the ferry boat bore them all away; they went out of the lighted gangway into the night; and we cheered them away, for the sake of the noise.

After this, we went down to the orlop for Divisions. The deck looked strange without the lines of sea chests; even the heaps of gear usually to be found "behind chests" were gone; it looked always most noble and ship-like, when stripped bare thus. Each man had now nothing but a hand-bag containing his night- and washing-gear. I had expected a night of war-path and disorder; with pitchings-out and cuttings-down. In this, I was wrong. The last night of term was never rowdy; it was, if anything, quiet. A good many men came round to say good-bye. Many of the Quarter Boys came trooping along; they were come to say good-bye to Dick and Red Swab, but their hearts were a little torn, many of them spoke friendly words to the new chums, who, but a few days before, had been the unspeakables, the untouchables, who were not even cannon fodder, but so many eyes to be ——

It must have been late when we turned in; we were all too much excited to bother about that; we knew, that long before the morning, we should be piped up, and away aboard a tug for the Liverpool Stage.

In a few minutes, as it seemed, the pipe went for 'All Hands', and the C.P.O. gave the long-hoped-for call of three cheers for going home *today*. We gave those cheers, and then, away, away, with gaiety and kindness, we lashed and stowed, and rushed to the lavatory. Old hands no longer seemed to need seven basins, but let the new chum wash, as if he were a man and a brother. It was a pitch dark morning, about five o'clock in mid December. We were piped to breakfast, but who wanted breakfast; there were the pats of butter, but who wanted butter? We wanted the tug, which now drew near under her navigation lights, and sidled in below the port gangway. With a few last good-byes we edged away, down the steps into the tug. It was most bitterly cold and pitch dark, with few lights moving on the River.

I looked up from the tug at the ship. The ports were all more or less lit; and heads showed from some of the ports; a cook or two, forward, an Instructor, perhaps; then, further aft, the heads of Masters, who opened up, and called to some of us.

The Skipper and Officers were at the gangway top.

The navigation bell rang; the tugmen were casting off, and the blades were thrashing. Our C.P.O. called for three cheers for the Captain, and so, with those, and other cheers, for Ship, Masters and Instructors, the tug got her fasts aboard, sidled, somehow, clear, and then clanged for full ahead. In a moment she had stridden clear of the ship and set her course down the Sloyne; the term was over.

Some of our men had left the ship in rags of old uniforms. I had wondered at this, for most of us had smartened up for going home. Now I saw that these men were stripping off their rags and putting on "serges." They had left the ship, and were taking off the marks of her; their rags, they flung overboard, or were flinging overboard when the tugmen begged for them. With a clink of money jingled in a cap the C.P.O. cried: "Come on, all hands, remember the tugmen." He passed among us, making up a collection; we all gave something, for they were taking us home.

I had never before been along the River in the dark;

to me, the voyage was one of the deepest beauty; the cities were asleep on the banks, and the liners at their moorings. It was all so silent, but for our engines and the washing by of water. Lairds' great gantries were silent; not a riveter at work yet. The roar of a seaport's daily labour, which I had so often noticed when aloft, was not begun for the day. Some ships lay under riding lights, and one or two small things went by with lights; police boats, we said, on River Patrol.

In the pitch darkness, we drew near the lights of the Stage and slackened for coming alongside. I love watching the skill of men; I have for years watched the skill of men who handle tugs, and ferries and bring them alongside piers just as gently as though the ships were made of egg-shell. We all watched the skill of our tug-men, who, in the darkness, crept to a berth and stopped at invisible marks by a sense which none of us had. A big man, who was leaving, clapped me on the shoulder. "Just the very same spot where we stopped, at the end of my first term," he said. "The very same. Good-bye, chum." I had dreaded him all through the term, for he was a bit of a terror to youth; now, here he was, sentimental. I shook hands with him and said good-bye. I was to meet him again more than forty years later. I remembered him well; he had no recollection of me whatsoever; what is a new chum, that an old hand should consider him?

Our ship's company cheered the tugmen; then the gangway came down, and we passed ashore, and in an instant ceased to be a ship's company. Nearly all the men melted away in gangs towards the big Liverpool stations. I was not starting from Liverpool. I had some hours to wait; then I had to take a ferry across the river to Woodside. I was left quite alone on the Landing Stage, with nothing to do but keep warm. For a time, I watched the River; then, as it began to be light, I walked out to the docks, past the ships for sale; and in the grey of the morning came upon a mate and apprentice washing down the deck of a small full-rigged ship. I asked if I might come aboard and bear a hand. The mate said: "Yes, if you're such a —— fool."

I suppose I was, for I went, and bore a hand; it was interesting to me to be doing the real thing. The apprentice was a big, easy, red-haired fellow. The mate asked me what the hell I was coming to sea for; to see the beautiful lands? I said: "Yes, sir." He said he supposed there must always be fools in the world.

We were finishing the work, which had been nearly finished when I joined them, when I saw a tug coming towards us in the dock, shifting the berth of a small barque. It was clear to me at once, that this barque's topsail yards would foul the chain maintopsail sheets of the ship. I said to the mate: "She'll foul you, sir, won't she?" He said: "No"; but she did; we had to run, and cast off the falls from the pin, and then race up to overhaul them and pitch them clear. This was a thrilling instant to me; I was out on a real main yard, helping in a real event.

After this, I started to see some more ships, and presently went aboard a small and very filthy steamer. I had never been aboard such a ship, and wished to see what she was like. She had come in about an hour before, but was apparently deserted save for a watchman, who very kindly showed me the sights. I asked him if I might see the focsle. He said: "This is where the men live," and opened to my view a sort of small, frowsy, bare iron box, with a wet floor and a few wooden shelves. The ship had probably taken a sea aboard while crossing the bar that morning. I know that my young heart sank, at the thought that that box was the home of men for days together, and that those wooden shelves were their resting places, after their battling with the sea. I had seen many dogs, and many pigs, better housed; infinitely better, for the keepers of the pigs and dogs liked their beasts to lie dry, and provided bedding for them. The ship gave a floor, iron roof, iron walls, and a wooden shelf to sleep on.

I left this horrible ship with my young heart in a whirl. This was an appalling world, that I had come into, if this were the thing given for faithful service. I remembered the phrase from *Treasure Island:* "Never saw good come of it yet. Spoil focsle hands, make devils." I asked myself: "Well, what do you make if you treat focsle hands much worse than pigs or dogs? Angels, perhaps? You do not make them happy men, and what sort of a man do you show yourself in the process?"

It was light, now, and the ferries were running; people were flooding into the city from the Stage, so I turned slowly past the ships for sale, and judged which I would buy if I had the money, and how much she would cost, and where the snag would be; for probably each had something wrong with her, and I wondered how you began to test an iron ship for sea-worthiness. In a wooden ship, as I knew full well, she let in the water and showed you, and when you docked her, you saw where her copper had given. I noticed, and remembered, some little points of rigging, as signs of age; single topsails on mizen masts; dead-eyes and laniards (sometimes with most exquisite paunch mattings covering the laniards), and the big, rigged-in, jibbooms and flying jibbooms, the sailor killers, which mates would have to rig out, with four boys and a drunken boatswain, on the way down River, outward bound.

I never failed to be stirred by the view southward from that now vanished dock. You could not see the River, for sheds, buildings, and our beloved Baths were in the way; instead of the river, you saw a kind of lightening in the sky in which a gull or two might shine; you knew that the River was there, with all its glory of beauty. I had not dreamed that any place could be so beautiful; I went towards it, knowing that I should see a new view of it, under an early morning sun. In a few minutes, I was looking at it from this new setting, of sunrise. I took careful observations of the movements of the clouds; those were interesting to me; the ships were beautiful; their building and rigging were wonderful to me. It was, however, quite clear to me, that something was very much amiss somewhere; there was too much grab, too much snatch, and I knew very well, that I did not want to belong to it. I wanted to be clear of the type of man who gave iron walls and a shelf, and a little daily offal, in exchange for a life's work. Then, with H.B. and Bill both gone, what would the ship be like in the next half?

Pondering these things, and profoundly saddened by the thought of that awful focsle, and the further thought, that the seamen from it were now probably drunk and being robbed by such harpies as I had seen besetting seamen, I took the ferry across. Somehow I always think that the Woodside ferry-boat bells are sweeter than any bells, at any rate they were, in those days, in the southward journey, when I was going home.